Aristotle's Guide
to Self-Persuasion

ALSO BY JAY HEINRICHS

Thank You for Arguing

How to Argue with a Cat

Word Hero

Aristotle's Guide to Self-Persuasion

How Ancient Rhetoric,
Taylor Swift, and Your Own Soul
Can Help You Change Your Life

JAY HEINRICHS

CROWN
NEW YORK

CROWN
An imprint of the Crown Publishing Group
A division of Penguin Random House LLC
1745 Broadway
New York, NY 10019
crownpublishing.com
penguinrandomhouse.com

Copyright © 2025 by Jay Heinrichs
Penguin Random House values and supports copyright. Copyright fuels creativity, encourages diverse voices, promotes free speech, and creates a vibrant culture. Thank you for buying an authorized edition of this book and for complying with copyright laws by not reproducing, scanning, or distributing any part of it in any form without permission. You are supporting writers and allowing Penguin Random House to continue to publish books for every reader. Please note that no part of this book may be used or reproduced in any manner for the purpose of training artificial intelligence technologies or systems.

CROWN and the Crown colophon are registered trademarks of
Penguin Random House LLC.

Library of Congress Cataloging-in-Publication Data is on file with the publisher.

Hardcover ISBN 978-0-593-73527-5
International edition ISBN 979-8-217-08628-3
Ebook ISBN 978-0-593-73528-2

Editor: Matt Inman
Assistant Editor: Fariza Hawke
Production editor: Craig Adams
Text designer: Amani Shakrah
Production: Heather Williamson
Copy editor: Mimi Lipson
Proofreaders: Chris Jerome and Pam Rehm
Indexer: J S Editorial, LLC
Publicist: Lindsay Cook
Marketers: Julie Cepler and Hannah Perrin

Manufactured in the United States of America

9 8 7 6 5 4 3 2 1

First Edition

The authorized representative in the EU for product safety and compliance is Penguin Random House Ireland, Morrison Chambers, 32 Nassau Street, Dublin D02 YH68, Ireland, https://eu-contact.penguin.ie.

To Viyan, and to her life's argument from strength.

Contents

Introduction
    Leave the Rut
        The useful art of soul bending   1

PART 1: Readiness

1 | Soul
    Motivate Yourself
        Hamlet's most excellent question   13

2 | Kairos
    Pluck the Day
        A timely exploration of the land of Serendib   25

3 | Inspiration
    Find Illumination
        Muses, molecules, and other means of great ideas   46

4 | Hyperbole
    Blow Things Up
        JFK's lunar trope   60

PART 2: Grasp

5 | Ethos
Trust Yourself
- Ben Franklin's chastity experiment 77

6 | Pathos
Control Your Mood
- Caesar's hilarious compendium of jokes 92

7 | Logos
Come to Believe
- Taylor Swift's rational color 108

8 | Framing
Define Your Life
- Rhetoric's loose-handled spade 124

PART 3: Action

9 | Habit
Adjust Your Routine
- Aristotle's Tortoise Method 143

10 | Charms
Change the Voice in Your Head
- The Forever Diamond and other reality benders 158

11 | Narrative
Tell Your Story
- Aristotle's enchanting knots 185

12 | Experimentation
Test the Tools
- An exemplarily stupid and pointless feat 202

PART 4: Solution

13 | Joy
Find Happiness
Why the lama giggled   213

14 | Peroration
Tap the Power of Words
The why of being human   228

THE TOOLS	235
FURTHER READING	251
ACKNOWLEDGMENTS	263
INDEX	265

Aristotle's Guide to Self-Persuasion

Introduction

Leave the Rut

The useful art of soul bending

"Wish is a form of appetite..."

—Aristotle, *On the Soul*

This book got its start some years ago when I attempted to turn my life around with rhetoric, the art of persuasion. To be honest, my wife, Dorothy, told me to. She's very smart and I do everything she says; so, tapping the wisdom of Aristotle and other sages, I began an ambitious experiment in self-persuasion.

The art itself began in the most social of ways, when a bevy of ancient consultants in Greece got rich by helping people win lawsuits and rule the masses through the sheer power of words. These itinerant experts deftly branded themselves "the Wise Ones"—*Sophists*. One of them, a massively popular Greek orator named

Gorgias (exquisitely pronounced "gorgeous") made so much money speaking and teaching rhetoric that he allegedly ordered a solid gold statue of himself. It was as if Taylor Swift supplemented her enormous concert revenues by teaching songwriting . . . and then erected a gold statue of herself.

Over the centuries, rhetoric went on to inspire democracies, lubricate business deals, and build empires. It empowered the likes of Lincoln and Gandhi and MLK. The American Founders used their common schooling in rhetoric to help throw off the yoke of empire and launch a republic. Shakespeare applied the knowledge of rhetoric he acquired at the Stratford Grammar School to do, well, Shakespeare. One of the original liberal arts, rhetoric is partly responsible for what we know as western civilization.

Rhetoric does more than win friends and influence people. The Sophists claimed it can bewitch an audience with the practice of *psychagogia,* or "soul moving." (The ancient Romans more aptly called it soul *bending.*) The gorgeous Greek Gorgias credited rhetoric with moving the soul of beautiful Helen, along with her body, all the way to Troy—launching those thousand ships and sparking the Trojan War. Gorgias played her defense attorney in a mock trial, blaming rhetoric for "drugging" her.

Some years ago, my wife became weirdly convinced that rhetoric's power could help me personally. Dorothy is the kind of dawn-enabled lark who springs out of bed with a cheerful "Good morning! What are your plans for the day?" and I love her anyway. I, on the other hand, am by nature the kind of geezer we used to make fun of, resenting the state of the world and kids these days. What's more, back then I was suffering from an ailment called snapping hip syndrome, which begins with a debilitating tightening up of the muscles. You could say the same thing was going on with the rest of me. In my late fifties, I had gotten old beyond my years, drinking too much and growing nostalgic for the good old days when I was an enthusiastic outdoorsman. Worst of all, I was losing my taste for life. I was truly stuck.

A relentless booster, Dorothy listed some of the triumphs that had come from my work with the art of rhetoric: helping pediatricians get children vaccinated, enabling NASA to coax mothballed MX missiles from the Pentagon, showing corporations how to recover from their own screwups . . .

She leaned in and whispered ecstatically, "And you once got thousands of publishing executives to lick each other!" (This was not entirely accurate. I had *asked* two thousand executives to lick each other. It was in the London Palladium during a tour for my book *How to Argue with a Cat*. The stage lights were bright, and I couldn't see the audience. But I did get them to purr.)

Still, Dorothy believed that my work on the ancient art lacked one helpful angle. "Have you thought of using the tools on yourself?"

I shook my head. It was true that whole empowering philosophies—Stoicism and Epicureanism, among others—had been built from the foundations of rhetoric. But rhetoric requires an audience; it stands to reason. Besides, persuasion works best when it disguises itself. No one likes to be manipulated. What kind of persuasion succeeds when both manipulator and manipulatee are the same person? It would be like a magician revealing his fakery during the performance. *Here's the woman's torso and the box that doesn't really cut her in half!*

Dorothy ignored my objections. "What have you got to lose?"

With frequent nudging by my wife, I did a deep dive into Aristotle, poring over works that I had passed by in my previous rhetorical research, and . . . eureka. Self-persuasion has an audience after all. It's not you, exactly; not the you who scarfs potato chips and binge-watches streaming shows. It's your very own soul.

I don't necessarily mean the immortal spirit we hear about in churches and temples, but rather Aristotle's brilliantly distinct concept of a soul. In his view, your soul is a superior version of yourself, one that reflects your truest character and reason for being. Your Aristotelian soul is your you-est you, the Michael Jackson man-in-the-mirror. It can become your audience, enabling you to bend it as the ancients liked to say. By directing rhetorical devices at this "audience," you could master another language, change careers, or simply overcome a fear of heights. The process makes you more resilient, better at dealing with change, and more skilled at growing old with grace. Most of all, rhetorical soul bending offers *agency*—the power to change your character from victim to protagonist, allowing you to take control of your brain and your circumstances. It lets you be the boss of you.

How can an art created by dead white men be relevant today? The ancients knew that, while cultures change, human nature remains the same. You'll find the lessons of persuasion woven through politics, literature, philosophy, and even popular culture—and many of its teachers appear in this book. Aristotle, Socrates, Benjamin Franklin, Hedy Lamarr, Muhammed Ali, P. T. Barnum, Jeffrey "the Dude" Lebowski, and of course Taylor Swift will help illustrate the concepts. Their wisdom literally got me off the couch.

Count the Ways

Obviously, you don't need a particular goal to practice the art of rhetoric on yourself. As far as we know, Aristotle never assigned himself any specific goals. (*Get tutoring job, teach young prince how to conquer world.*) Still, a good project offers a chance to experiment, not just with the tools but with yourself. Plus, if friends notice a change in you, imagine the frisson you can experience when you tell them your success has something to do with the Aristotelian concept of the soul.

Here are a few examples of where this book might take you. Your first project may be to dream up a specific goal of your very own, one that best suits your yearning soul. (Turn to chapter three for rhetorical inspiration.)

Lose weight. In attempting any objective, we need to know the *frame,* ensuring that we firmly grasp the meaning of the terms. What exactly does losing weight mean to you? While we're pondering the definition of our issue, we might as well throw in a logical analysis, assessing the goal with an ancient system that inspired the scientific method. Before we start starving ourselves, though, we want to get in touch with our soul, which you'll meet in the next chapter. If all this framing and assessing seem like a pain, put it this way: The time you spend on thinking is a hiatus from all that diet and exercise.

Learn a new skill. Let's say you want to play the guitar. You do some online research, buy the instrument, and schedule lessons. What else do you need to do? How much persuasion does it take to do something you have always wanted to do? Well, obviously, the problem is not playing the guitar. It's practicing the guitar. This is true for any new skill—learning a language, taking up fly-fishing, or mastering haute cuisine. The idea sounds brilliant until it comes to finding an hour a day and then going through the necessary repetitive motions, bleeding fingers, and tedium. A variety of tools in this book will give you the motivation to keep going.

Give a speech. This ambition is not at all impressive if you were born a natural ham, free of any performance anxiety. Just write a good text and, ideally, memorize it. For the rest of us, though, we need to deal with our fear. Start with a mindset—or *frame,* in rhetoric—that redefines the occasion as something less scary. *It's a toast, not a State of the Union Address.* You will master redefinition in chapter seven.

Become wittier. The ability to speak or write cleverly can do wonders for boosting confidence or overcoming shyness. In chapter nine, you'll find ways to express even the most mundane thoughts in ways that make people (and yourself) think you're terribly clever. Admittedly, Aristotle dismissed wit as "educated arrogance." But he himself would have benefited from a wittier style. While his thoughts are profoundly brilliant, reading them entails a terrible slog. You and I will never become Aristotles, but we can make ourselves more entertaining through cunning rhetorical devices.

Improve your love life. This objective admittedly sounds cringingly self-helpish; but ancient philosophers wrote volumes on sex and relationships. (Socrates being an exception; when he lost his sex drive in old age, he told friends he was glad to be "rid of an old demon." Was his wife just as grateful?)

You can find whole taxonomies of love in the literature. Search for "Aristotle's Masterpiece" on the Web, and up pops an English sex manual, first published in 1684 and falsely attributed to the philosopher. The pseudonymous author had good reason to borrow the brand; Aristotle had written at least two books covering reproduction in animals. The modern reader would hardly think the man wrote the book on human love. For one thing, Aristotle believed that the female was, "as it were, a deformed male." Still, given that Aristotelian rhetoric starts with the tools to gain the liking and trust of people, we had best not dismiss him right away.

But this is a book of self-persuasion, not of Marvin-Gaye-get-it-on seduction. In order to gain a lover or improve a relationship with a significant other, we need to begin by seducing ourselves—convincing our disappointed souls that we are worthy of love. Just about every tool in this book applies.

Learn to nap. While this goal may not seem terribly ambitious, it requires as much rhetorical skill as any other venture. Most people who fail to take a daily rest will tell you, "I don't nap." Well, of course. This is literally true. Those among us with demanding in-person jobs find few opportunities to put their feet up and snooze. But over years of napless days, *I don't nap* can turn into a self-description, as in *I'm not the type who naps*. At that point, even the best circumstances for napping—remote work, quiet room, long lunch hour—won't lead to one of the finest habits to promote health and sanity. Your false interpretation of your soul gets in the way. In the next chapter, we'll work to fix that problem. Then, to foster the habit yourself, you can call upon a whole rhetorical array, from framing to Aristotle's Lure & Ramp method.

In fact, I would argue that the napping skill can constitute the single greatest proof of your ability to persuade yourself. Now there's ambition for you.

Set your own goal. Start a business, buy your first home, earn another degree, quit smoking, learn a language, read *Moby-Dick* for pleasure . . . Every ambitious objective uses similar rhetorical methods. You can find inspiration in chapter three. Then align your ambition with your soulful needs and consider a wildly ambitious goal. Whether you triumph or fail nobly, your effort will allow you to see a more soulful person, a decorous *ethos*, in the mirror.

Navigating Change

The tools of rhetoric start with improving your mood, your self-beliefs, and your willingness to take action—or to stop doing something harmful. *Changing your mood* can be relatively easy. Take a bath, light a candle, watch cat videos. The effect rarely lasts, but you will have succeeded in a small rhetorical victory. Changing your default mood, on the other hand—transforming your habitual emotional state—takes some serious self-persuasion.

Changing your mind is less easy. You know this from the horrible political fights that ruin Thanksgiving dinner. Still, with the right rhetorical tools, you can succeed in a self-consensus favoring Dunkin' Donuts coffee over Starbucks; or an apple over a donut.

Now, *action*—persuading yourself to exercise at an ungodly hour, or to eliminate cocktail hour—comes hardest of all. You can download a jaunty exercise playlist and win an argument with yourself about the need to get fit; but actually doing the crunches you intended? Gym franchises' whole business plans depend on your failure to show up. The tools in this book can spark the motivation you need. A couple of them can even remove the need for motivation altogether. They will help you get unstuck and gain triumphant goals, both ambitious and merely healthy.

Obviously, this book will not replace therapy or cure neuroses. But if you end up in a rut, you probably struggle to talk yourself out of it. One reason could be your own self-identity—your *ethos*, in rhetoric. In my persuasion consulting practice, I often hear young clients say, "I'm not a leader." Out-of-shape men and women often reveal that they "don't sweat." And I once had a friend share that he would love to learn guitar but that he was "not musical," as if he had inherited a chord-blocking gene. Sure, he might never cut an album, but with the appropriate rhetorical tools he should be able to learn to strum a decent "I Fought the Law," and feel good about that.

All the tools in this book have to do with the ways our minds process words. Early on, the Sophists understood that they could manipulate their audiences' perception of reality. In the chapters to come, you'll see that the Sophists' techniques led to pure magic, transforming existence through the repeated use of certain terms. In learning these tools yourself, you might change your own meaning—your life's essential cause.

This is more than a revenue source for me; it happens to be my own cause. Used for good, rhetoric's tools of human manipulation bring people together, help them make mutual decisions, and inspire them to act. Used for evil . . . well. We all have seen what the dark art can do in politics and marketing, not to mention family relations. All the more reason to unveil the secrets.

In the meantime, we're changing ourselves. As an example, I will tell the tale of a rail-thin character standing almost naked in the early cold at the base of a mountain. He has talked himself into the notion that he is a magnificent athlete, that getting up in the dark is a fine habit, and that the silly goal that he will probably fail to achieve represents the single greatest idea he has ever had. His personal experiment includes a mountain, a diet, an exercise plan, a radical change of habits, a personal made-to-order time zone, thousands of embarrassing strangers, and a birthday. Not to mention his wife, thank her endlessly tolerant soul.

That character, of course, is me. Some of the tools in the experiment failed miserably. Others succeeded far beyond my expectations. My experiment literally changed my life. More importantly, what it taught me just might change yours.

Part 1

READINESS

1

Soul

Motivate Yourself

Hamlet's most excellent question

"Everyone ceases to inquire how he is to act when he has brought the moving principle back to himself and to the ruling part of himself . . ."

—Aristotle, *Nicomachean Ethics*

Successful self-persuasion worms through the gaps in life, or closes them altogether. There's the gap between our lust for a fresh, inviting cinnamon roll and our desire to lose a few pounds. Many of us sense a gap between the life we have grown accustomed to and the alarming changes we see around us—or within ourselves. In this chapter, Aristotle will help us deal with a more personal chasm: between your day-to-day self, the one salivating in front of that cinnamon roll, and your superior soul.

Personally, when I look in the mirror first thing in the morning,

I hardly see a fine human specimen. Yet effective rhetoric depends on getting your audience to like and trust you—projecting an upstanding character, or *ethos*. When that assembly consists solely of the person in the mirror, you literally face a problem. That mirror image can see right through you, flaws and past sins and all. It's the great self-persuasion paradox: To believe in yourself, you first have to get yourself to believe in yourself. Most of the devices in this book exist to help close that gap, the one that separates our noble core from our sorry daily behavior.

Scientist that he was, Aristotle pursued the concept of the soul like a biologist studying the liver. He speculated about the various parts of the body that might contain the soul. (Many years later, the seventeenth-century philosopher and devoted Aristotelian René Descartes located the soul precisely in the pineal gland.) Aristotle went on to ask: Was the soul "the rational faculty"—or, as we moderns would say, the mind? If so, was it made of something physical, or did the soul exist beyond our own bodies, "intermingled in the whole universe"? Aristotle seemed to be enjoying himself in these speculations. The soul can't exist everywhere, he decided, because plants do not have souls. Neither, he believed, do animals. This makes me doubt he had pets.

Therefore, Aristotle concluded, the soul had to be something human; not a physical object but a kind of spiritual spark plug, the quality of a person that senses things and responds to those sensations. The soul is the *you*-ness of a person, one's deepest identity and ultimate motive. Aristotle wrote an entire book on the soul—titled, appropriately, *On the Soul*—and devoted many thousands of words in his other books to the art of bending it.

While any attempt to persuade yourself aloud can seem positively schizophrenic, the soul provides the required audience. This helps explain why some people can talk themselves into good habits and noble goals. The "themselves" they convince are their souls. In return, their souls make them better.

Modern science rarely examines the soul; but you can see traces of Aristotle in many social science experiments. The noted psychologist Elliot Aronson called self-persuasion the most effective enticement of all. Other kinds of allurements, such as advertising or political speeches, often fail to persuade because they come from an external source. We see an ad telling us to vote for someone and we ask ourselves, "Do we really want to?" With self-persuasion, Aronson said, "individuals come to believe that they really want to." That's because they themselves wanted to in the first place. Then what was the need for persuasion? If you want to do something, why not follow the path of almighty Nike and just do it?

You know why: Desire only gets you so far. Aronson believed that your own sense of identity will take you much further. His research showed that *cognitive dissonance* triggers self-persuasion. This is the unpleasant feeling we get when we say or do something counter to our own beliefs—"especially if this action threatens the individual's self-concept of being a decent or rational person."

He and a colleague conducted an experiment in which they invited volunteers to join a discussion session. First, the scientists put half the group through a rigorous initiation; the other half suffered only a mild introduction. The psychologists who led the discussion deliberately made it boring. Afterward, the volunteers who had been through the mild initiation admitted they had been bored. The ones who had been through the tough version, on the other hand, were convinced that the discussion had been fascinating. They thought of themselves as rational people. What reasonable person would deliberately go through a torturous initiation just for a pointless conversation? The experiment had caused painful cognitive dissonance in those poor volunteers.

Aristotle would have understood the phenomenon. The participants' self-identity constituted what he called the soul. When each volunteer manipulated herself into believing that the discussion was interesting, she was trying to strike a harmonious chord with her soul.

Was this a good thing? Weren't the volunteers simply deluding themselves?

Welcome to the dark art of rhetoric. Aristotle, the most rational of all rational beings, understood that logic rarely persuades on its own. The most powerful persuasion comes from an audience's sense of its identity and its identification with the speaker. Any dissonance between the persuader and the audience, however logical the message, will block the persuasion. When it comes to persuading yourself, the audience is your soul. The more your daily behavior strays, the more you separate yourself from your soul's true needs. This, Aristotle would say, is a major source of unhappiness. Your soul and your behavior fail to strike a harmonious chord. When a parent says "You're better than this" to a naughty child, she points to what she optimistically believes to be an admirable little soul, one distinct from the kid's abominable behavior. When Taylor Swift sings to an ex-boyfriend "It's my turn to be me," the "me" is her true self—as opposed to the lovesick Taylor who, as she says in the same song, "bent all my rules." Ditto when she sings "I'm the only one of me." Good for her. This woman is in harmony with her own soul.

Your Soul Is a Scout

Think of your soul as the you your daily you rarely lives up to. It's the *higher* you, the one that restrains itself from finishing a quart of Cherry Garcia ice cream before bed. This admirable soul of yours does not have to be sweet-smelling and beautiful. Even Aristotle, who set very high soul standards, described the best kind of soul as a sort of ancient Boy Scout. (So much for sweet-smelling.) A good soul, he said, is:

Just, treating others fairly.

Courageous, occupying the perfect middle ground between cowardice and foolhardiness.

Restrained, naturally self-disciplined. One glass of wine is enough, thank you. The perfect soul never exceeds its budget.

Magnanimous, generous toward the deserving.

Liberal, being open to those souls that are unlike itself, and looking benignly if skeptically at novelty or change.

Prudent, making the right choices to suit every occasion, without getting all emotional about it.

And, best of all, Wise. It is large. It contains multitudes of knowledge and judgment.

Such a soul may not sound like much fun at a party, let alone easy to live with. But Aristotle recognized that the actions of real human beings never perfectly reflect their souls. The characters he admired most were the tragic heroes immortalized in plays; and even these good-looking, brave types were not relatable unless they came with some serious flaws.

If you get nothing else out of this book—if you choose not to come up with a particular goal, or have no habits you wish to reset—I hope you acquire the rhetorical frame of mind that boosts your self-liking and self-trust. Your noble soul deserves this.

My own soul happens to be . . . Well, this only seems like bragging, but my soul is pretty awesome. So, by definition, is yours. But the contrast between our souls and our daily actions can seem like an abyss. My soul has all the traits of a Boy Scout: trustworthy, loyal, helpful, friendly, courteous, kind, more or less obedient, cheerful, thrifty, brave, fairly clean, and, when it isn't making irreverent jokes, reverent. Plus: fit, athletic, good-looking, witty, brilliantly articulate, impressively knowledgeable, and ambitious for all the right reasons. That's my soul. As for my daily self . . . sigh. It's grouchy, timid, too lazy to shave, could lose a few pounds, and uses Thesaurus.com like an addict. So much for cheerful, brave, clean, athletic, and articulate. And don't get me started on the rest. My soul is light-years ahead of what I am from day to day. But that is the very purpose of having a soul and becoming aware of it.

Oh, sure, my soul has flaws of its own. It tends to be overly optimistic, too trusting of people, too much in love with its own ideas. And it can be pretty darn judgmental toward the mortal, regular, daily me. There are times when I want to get my soul drunk and make it say something embarrassing in front of respectable people. I'm not alone in this feeling. In Homer's *Odyssey*, the great Odysseus stages frequent debates between his tricky, selfish, daily character and his nobler self—his soul, as Aristotle would say later. Not even heroes get along with their souls all the time.

One trait of a noble soul can take us through our own stormy odysseys. According to the ancient Roman rhetorician and Aristotle fanboy Marcus Tullius Cicero, our ability to bear injustice and bad fortune is our saving grace. Our souls can stand a great deal. If Cicero had been next to Hamlet while he debated whether to be or not to be, the Roman would have had a ready answer. The melancholy Dane asks which is nobler: "to suffer the slings and arrows of outrageous fortune," or "to take arms against a sea of troubles." Suffer, Cicero would say. Definitely suffer. He meant that as a kind of skill—not a state of agony but a knack for withstanding it. Leaving aside the fact that carrying a sword into the sea hardly reveals a rational soul, Cicero would be making an important point. The ancients believed that our own inherited flaws and the horrible luck flung at us by outrageous fortune can serve as opportunities to demonstrate our souls' superior nobility.

That nobility was what Aristotle called *arete,* or virtue, a quality that, besides making others look up to you, can help you produce "many and signal good works." So let's discover that noble soul of yours.

Time to Sync Up

Some people seem to be in close touch with their souls almost from birth. Cassius Clay, long before he was Muhammed Ali, called himself the greatest of all time—long before he proved himself to be the greatest of all time. While New Age aficionados claim he "manifested" his future, Aristotle would say he synced up with his soul.

That syncing would not be necessary if we behaved nobly all the time. In fact, one of the best ways to define your noble soul is to list the ways you have separated from it. Why go to all this trouble merely to define the nobler part of you? Why not just list your eternal values and beliefs and construct an impression of your soul? The answer lies in rhetoric. We tend to express our values in *commonplaces:* terms that reflect the beliefs of the tribes we belong to. *I'm passionate for diversity. I believe in freedom. It takes a village.* There's nothing wrong with these values, of course. But things get weird when we try to define them. We see how complicated terms like *freedom* or *diversity* can be, and how each tribe gives them a different interpretation. This spoils the patriotic point of these expressions—as if we told a group of American patriots that "The Star Spangled Banner" is nothing more than terrible music set to a lousy poem.

Commonplaces often fail to define our deepest personal values. They just define our tribe. Aristotle would urge us to skip the words and think of our actions; and then assess how we felt afterward. Later on, we'll deal with how to manipulate our own emotions. For now, use your feelings to separate the soulful from the ignoble.

> Exercise: Think of the times you acted nobly: selflessly, capably, and grandly, living up to Aristotle's heroic ideal; or the Scouting ideal—whichever appeals to you. Write down these instances of nobility.
>
> Next, recall the times you behaved shamefully. What embarrassed you most? Try to assess exactly why you felt ashamed. Did you make a fool of yourself in front of others? Or did you do something that violated your own morals?
>
> Finally—and this will help you recover from that shaming task—list the times you suffered outrageous fortune. When did you respond well, bearing up under pressure, being the adult in hostile rooms, acting wisely or with courage when you had every reason to panic?

While most of us keep our shame to ourselves, social media makes it possible to track the best and worst behavior of every public character. Elon Musk, for example: No one has broadcasted extremes of nobility and ignobility more than this man. He seemed to become aware of his life's soulful purpose as a youth when he modestly decided to dedicate his life to saving the future of humanity. Musk's crazy impulsiveness may seem to get in the way of that admirable purpose (*I'll spend forty-four billion on a social media cesspool and turn it into a one-stop financial system that will . . . save the future of humanity!*); but you can't say the man lacks motivation. This chapter, remember, is all about motivation.

The interesting thing about Elon Musk from a rhetorical perspective is that, despite his vast wealth, he does not seem to be in it for the money. At least he's not into the kind of showy super-yacht lifestyle that the Amazonian Jeff Bezos favors. Bezos's soul seems made for money. You get a sense that, without his billions, Bezos simply would not be Bezos. Musk, on the other hand, wouldn't be Musk without Mars, or an all-electric future, or the chips he will someday implant in our brains to keep future robot overlords at bay and thus *save the future of humanity*! Money provides a means to that noble end. Meanwhile, he seems happy to sleep on the floor of a factory office, or in a modest house in the desert close to his beloved rockets. Don't expect him to serve as a lifestyle guru for the rest of us; he guzzles Red Bulls, and his sleep schedule seems nonexistent. But his daily actions clearly align with his admittedly weird soul.

While Musk may not provide the best role model, his life just might help you find your own soul. Where does he find the impulse to run six companies and get himself in all kinds of exciting trouble? Aristotle might say that his needs and wants are in sync. There is nothing cognitively dissonant about him.

To determine your final cause, it helps to separate your wants from your needs. Your wants tend to drive your daily choices, especially the ones you regret later. Your needs, on the other hand, reveal what you're *for*. Your needs are the means to your end—your final cause. Separating wants from needs can help you assay your Aristotelian soul. Determine the outline of that soul—your own most cherished, unique desire—and you will discover the spark that truly motivates it.

Skip the *Mona Lisa*

In this business of soul detecting, we should leave behind any assumptions about who we are, what role we play, or what society expects of us. To start with, try to determine the desires that come only from the sorts of things everybody does simply because everybody does it. If you keep a bucket list of places you want to explore, which items are ones that everybody in your tribe also tends to list? (While we're at it, do you really need a bucket list?)

Take the *Mona Lisa*, which would rank high in any bucket-list hall of fame. If you have been to the Louvre, you know what I mean. You enter a large room dedicated to that one picture—which is obscured by the horde of tourists jostling in front of it. Everybody is hopping up and down to get just enough of a glimpse so they can check the painting off their list. Meanwhile, not very far from that exhibit in the same museum, you can find a deserted room that contains Joyeuse, Charlemagne's sword. (Maybe that reveals more about me than you; I found the sword because I was drawn to an empty room.)

> Exercise: Think about the more memorable trips you have taken. Which of them never appear on travel web-

> sites or other people's social media? Because those sui generis adventures appeal to your deeper needs, distinct from the wants of social expectations, consider them to be hints emanating from your soul.

You might do the same want/need exercise with the books you read and the movies you watch. Not that you should avoid the popular books, but if you find yourself trudging through a text or sitting through a movie simply because it seems the right thing to do, then consider what book or movie you should pursue instead—one that might mark you as an eccentric. Somewhere in that pursuit, your soul is sending you faint pings.

If your soul is signaling unmet desires, that cognitive dissonance may have to do with the changes you see around you, not to mention the chaos of daily life. In the next chapter, you will find ways to deal with that chaos, and maybe even exploit it.

THE TOOL

<u>Soul Detector.</u> List the times you acted most "nobly," as Aristotle would put it—responding to the best instincts of your soul. What made you especially proud of the noble actions? What values did you live up to? If you write them down as adjectives, you will help describe what Aristotle calls your *soul*.

> Next, list the actions or desires that ignore societal roles and expectations. What strikes you as original or, even better, eccentric? What does that say about you?
>
> Third, try to separate your wants from your truest needs. This shouldn't make you feel guilty; if your

deepest need is to see yourself as the athlete you once were, and you keep giving in to junk food and Netflix, don't worry. In the pages to come, you will gain more tricks to get what you need. Meanwhile, just find your soul. This is task enough for now.

2

Kairos

Pluck the Day

A timely exploration of the land of Serendib

"Old people live in memory rather than in hope."

—Aristotle, *Rhetoric*

Several years ago on New Year's Eve, I stood with my wife and son in our frozen backyard, shooting miniature fireworks from a German-made toy gun. I had already made up my list of New Year's resolutions—eat more vegetables, drink less alcohol, make more money—and now it was time to celebrate.

When our modest fireworks ran out, I turned to go inside. One foot slid on a patch of ice while the other stayed anchored, causing the bones below my knee to spiral around each other and break. I collapsed with my left foot pointing in the wrong direction.

"My leg is broken," I told Dorothy and George, stating the obvious, and my resolutions broke with it. All my plans landed with me in a heap, and long before midnight, the coming year veered in an entirely different direction.

We've all had moments like this, when our best-laid plans go astray and our accustomed lives suddenly seem foreign. A death, a pregnancy, a layoff, or a single lurking patch of ice sends us caroming into a change we didn't expect or want.

If you're reading this, you *want* change. That normal life you're living is not quite enough. But the change you don't enact for yourself is rarely the kind you want, and it happens constantly. We're stuck in a world that keeps moving without us. When we resolve to make a change on our own, we get swept up and dropped by the swirling chaos.

Our ancestors would roll their eyes at a statement like that. True, life was simpler in one respect: Most people were in no position to change it. Choices complicate things. If you were among the great majority who lived the way society or their masters dictated, then you spent less time agonizing over decisions. You lived where, and how, you were supposed to. Your daily routines were preordained. You certainly wouldn't need a book like this, assuming you could read.

A few people in ancient times did have choices, though. In cities like Athens, a significant minority were literate landowners, merchants, aristocrats, or all three. If you think *their* lives were simple, read the literature they left behind. They make *Game of Thrones* seem like a Jane Austen novel: invasions, rapes, poisonings, fratricides, political shenanigans, treaties made and almost immediately broken, trade routes carved out and then blocked. And that's just Athens and Sparta, the two leading cities in Greece's so-called Golden Age. You want chaos? They had chaos.

While few of us moderns are busy poisoning our enemies, we have an agency at least equal to those of ancient aristocrats; which means our lives are equally complex. So we'll want to see how our clever forebears dealt with life's inevitable chaos—not just the slip-and-fall emergencies but the daily swirling confusion of work and relationships, children and money and illness . . . oh my. Could the ancients have found some way to navigate through the madness—and somehow make the changes we want?

They could and did. Educated Greeks, along with scholarly Jews, developed an entire philosophy of chaos, one that can help you focus on your goals and even turn bad luck into potential opportunities.

While we moderns think of chaos as swirling confusion—tornadoes, tsunamis, small children—our forebears' biblical, pre-beginning Chaos was a formless void. The Sophists described it as a gloomy, dark, blank, pre-time place. The Greek word *khaos,* in fact, comes from the verb *khasko,* "to gape." The early Christians borrowed this concept, seeing chaos as a "great gulf" (*chaos magnum*) that separated heaven and hell.

Chaos, in other words, is more than just confusion. In the eyes of the ancients, it constitutes a mysterious gap. Taking the concept a natural step further, they understood that another way to interpret chaos is to see it as an opening—a doorway or window. The most confusing times also happen to be the most liminal, lying between more settled periods in our lives. Remember your teenage years? Chaos, totally magnum. Aristotle argued that any significant change in our lives, bad or good, constitutes a soul test.

Bad news, good news: Stuff happens. Your response determines what kind of soul you have, and how much you live up to that soul.

Even better, fortune and its resulting chaos can help us determine the best route to happiness. So let us discover the ways to spot an opportunity within a chaotic gap. It's where we find serendipity.

The Case of the Missing Camel

Once upon a time, the king of a rich land reached the sorry conclusion that his sons had been spoiled rotten. These privileged young jerks were taking their great wealth and status for granted. To teach them a permanent lesson, he banished them to a strange, hostile, faraway place.

Soon after they arrived, the young princes learned that a camel had gone missing. Having nothing else to do, they decided to investigate. After searching through clues at the scene of the crime, they reported their findings to the beast's owner, a merchant. "Your camel was old," one prince said. The second prince said, "It was missing a tooth and blind in one eye, carrying a load of honey on one side and butter on the other." "Plus a woman," the third prince added. "She was pregnant."

"Thieves!" the merchant shouted. "How can you know all that unless you stole the camel yourselves?" Outraged townsfolk dragged the princes before the emperor, and the merchant demanded their execution for the capital crime of camel rustling.

We interrupt this story to provide a crucial detail: The land where the princes had been banished, and where they were about to get their heads chopped off, was an empire called Serendib (now Sri Lanka). It's where we get the word *serendipity*: a happy chance occurrence. This admittedly makes no sense until you hear the rest of the tale.

The emperor gazed down from his throne at the princes. "What do you have to say for yourselves?" The boys explained that they had induced their facts from elementary observation. Grass had been eaten on the less lush side of the road, which had to mean the camel was blind on one side. Tooth-sized clumps of grass had been left behind, implying the missing tooth. Other clues included dribbles of fly-covered butter on one side and honey on the other, as well as a woman-sized footprint with two handprints in front of it, and a wet spot that smelled of urine. "It is obvious," the first prince said. "A woman had stopped to relieve herself and had to use her hands to get back up, which tells us that she was pregnant."

Just then, a man entered the palace, serendipitously shouting, "Is someone missing a camel?" He had found one wandering in the desert.

The delighted emperor showered the princes with gold and took them on as his top advisors. They all lived happily ever after, with the possible exception of the pregnant woman. Immortalized in a popular tale, "The Three Princes of Serendib," the adventure eventually inspired the Sherlock Holmes stories.

The moral, at least for our purposes: While we tend to think of opportunity as sheer luck, the greatest chances for success rarely arise in the best of times. Serendib is a scary, chaotic place where you could lose your head, but it's also the land of possibility.

Still, Aristotle would say that chaos is nothing but a gap in your life until you use it. When you begin to think serendipitously, you see chaos all around, in your own life as well as in popular culture. In the movie *It's a Wonderful Life*, Jimmy Stewart saves a building and loan while the evil Mr. Potter takes over the rest of the town. Some years later, Potter offers Stewart's character a job running his business. During the Depression, Potter says, "you and I were the only ones that kept our heads." The Potter-Stewart spirit seemed to hold true during the Covid-19 pandemic, when hopeful unemployed workers attempted to turn a disaster into a positive; new business applications for the year were up more than 43 percent.

An opportunity constitutes a fulcrum between outcomes. Your decision tips the scale and launches you into a particular future. While opportunity often entails good luck, just as often it means bad luck. Without the decision to investigate the camel mystery, the princes of Serendib would simply have suffered banishment.

Americans faced a fulcrum of their own when the Soviets shockingly sent up beeping, spiky little Sputnik, the first satellite. We responded with the fabulously ambitious Apollo program, going way beyond Earth's orbit and creating much of the technology that now enables our smartphones. We made the moon our Serendib. Kanye West became Taylor Swift's Serendib when he humiliated the nineteen-year-old singer at the MTV VMA awards; she rose to a whole new level of artistry. A Massachusetts printer named Milton Bradley landed on his own Serendib when he faced the looming bankruptcy of his printing company during a nineteenth-century economic depression. He dreamed up a game called The Game of Life, printed it, and launched the board game industry.

In the art of persuasion, the in-between times of opportunity are the *persuasive moments,* when an audience has not yet made up its mind and a choice must be made. A problem or gap needs a solution, and the time is ripe to sway people toward the decision you want. It's a time of *crisis*—a word that once had a more positive meaning than it does today. Bear with me for a bit more etymology.

We get our notion of crisis from the Greek *krisis*, meaning "decision." The Greeks labeled a persuadable moment *hypokrisis*, literally "before the decision." They saw decisions as a matter of contingency, applying wit and knowledge to solve singular problems and act on particular opportunities.

The same is true of every major decision—when to marry, when to buy a house, whether to quit your job and start a business. Serendipity lies at the beating heart of decisions.

Horace's Joy of Day Plucking

In the darkest times, paradigms shift. The Sophists entered Athens at just such a time. The city-state's government had evolved from a series of tyrannies to an unprecedented democracy. The tyrants had spent happy years stealing the homes of their enemies and granting them to friends. Now, in this crazy new time, real estate was a mess. Citizens were disputing titles in court, and there were no lawyers. For many, their chance to reclaim their home, or to avoid losing it to an opponent, came down to their own eloquence. Enter the Sophists. The chaos gave them an opening to sell an entire culture on the wonders of rhetoric.

Recognizing that chaotic openings were a kind of resource, the Sophists expanded the concept into a whole philosophy of opportunity. They called it **kairos** and defined it as an art of grabbing a moment at its ripest. When the rhetorically educated poet Horace wrote "*Carpe diem*," he didn't mean "Seize the day," exactly. A better translation might be "Pluck the day." You want to bite into an opportunity like a pear before it spoils. A ripe occasion is what rhetoricians call a kairotic moment. It's a time of change, of decision, a frontier lying between reality and possibility.

The tool of kairos helps you hunt through temporal gaps. In fact, the very word "opportunity" comes from the Latin *porta*, meaning "entrance" or "passage through." Ancient Greeks saw kairos as the art of piercing those openings. They described it as an arrow finding its way through an enemy's armor, or a weaver shoving the shuttle through the opening between warp and woof. The modern rhetorician Eric Charles White defined kairos as "a passing instant when an opening appears which must be driven through with force if success is to be achieved." Kairos, in other words, means navigating a void.

True story: Years ago, when my son, George, was thirteen, he and I went on a twenty-mile day hike in New Mexico. After trekking for hours through stark white desert, we suddenly found ourselves between rock walls. A waterfall splashed into a stream that bisected the canyon, fingerling trout hovered in the deeper water, and bright flowers grew from every crevice. I searched the map for the canyon and found nothing but desert where we were supposed to be. "We're lost," I said. "I'll climb the mesa and see if I can spot Los Alamos."

"That would be cheating," George said. So we walked on, and before long the canyon flattened out and we were back on the map. After ten minutes, I turned around. All desert. The canyon had disappeared. We named it Brigadoon Canyon after the story and musical about the Scottish town that appears once every hundred years.

George's mother solved the mystery after we got home. The map showed the topography in fifty-foot isobars; Brigadoon Canyon's walls were no higher than forty feet. Still, we declared the place to be magical. George's decision to keep walking without a map was like passing into a different, albeit tiny, universe. We might just as well have called the place Serendib.

In fact, Serendib, a slice of chaotic time, rarely comes with a map. Serendipity exists in an in-between space where the rules seem topsy-turvy or vanish altogether. The ancient Jews and early Christians described the universe before the Creation in this way. Before the beginning, there was Chaos. When the beginning began, according to the New Testament book of John, there was *Logos*.

Later in this book, you will see how to use rhetorical logos to manipulate logic. While Bible translators usually render *Logos* as "the Word," a more accurate version would be "rational thinking" or "strategy." *In the beginning was the plan.* John was an educated Roman citizen who had been taught to think kairotically. He understood that every great creation, including the original Creation, begins with a plan to fill a void.

The Bible's Ecclesiastes is a kairotic poem ("To everything there is a season, and a time to every purpose under Heaven"). A comedian who jokes about a tragedy and then asks, "Too soon?" acknowledges kairos. When an officer at the Battle of Bunker Hill said, "Don't fire until you see the whites of their eyes," he was being kairotic. *Strike while the iron is hot. Make hay while the sun shines. Time and tide wait for no man.* Many of our best clichés are kairotic.

Kairotic moments often come during a time of paradigm malfunction, when the usual norms no longer apply. Einstein noticed that Newtonian physics failed to solve the problems of the universe beyond our solar system. Adam Smith realized that his rapidly industrializing culture was no longer bound by the ties of nobility. As the philosopher Thomas Kuhn put it, these exceptional men were able to deal "with a world out of joint."

In the best of times—those rare seasons when your part of the world seems perfectly in joint—most of us bask in all that fortune and think it will last forever. When the stock market is soaring, people buy stocks. Back in the nineties, when dot-coms looked like the Next Big Thing, investors flocked to them. Snowbirds literally flock to Florida in the winter, when the weather is perfect. None of these actions seizes on a genuine opportunity. To be skillfully kairotic, you need to be somewhat contrarian, the Fool on the Hill who defies common sense by interpreting the sunset as the world spinning round. We have to think different. Common sense and normal thinking rarely detect the big, life-changing opportunities.

When scholars rediscovered ancient rhetorical texts in the seventeenth century, they used this situational thinking, this idea of gaps between belief and reality, to help form the scientific method. The modern philosopher Stephen Toulmin explains that science exists to fill chaotic gaps. "The gap between . . . explanatory ideals and actualities," he writes, "is a measure of the explanatory distance this particular science still has to go." In other words, when reality fails to back up a current scientific theory or contradicts our general understanding of nature, science has an obligation to fill the gap.

Actually, just such a gap inspired modern chaos theory. During the 1930s, a Dartmouth math major named Edward Lorenz got addicted to pinball. Soon after, town authorities banned the game, declaring it a form of gambling. The players relied on luck, they said, not skill. Lorenz—a passionate pinball player who deeply felt the loss of the game—knew that the authorities were wrong; the better players won more often than not. Still, Lorenz realized that skill did not make as much of a difference as statistics would predict. The caroming pinball introduced an element that could not be explained by either luck or skill. Lorenz devoted the rest of his life to exploring the gap. "The result was chaos," he said. He turned a gap in his own life—the loss of his favorite hobby—into a science of gaps.

Chaos opens up during caroming events. We tend to think that the greatest opportunities come from new discoveries—recent inventions, groundbreaking medicines, scientific breakthroughs, and the like. But as the political economist Joseph Schumpeter pointed out, the greatest fortunes get made by people who reap the whirlwind that swirls from the chaos of technological change. Bridges destroy ferry businesses while aiding truck farmers, who get wiped out by industrial agriculture, which in turn helps birth the Chicken McNugget. Computers replace typewriters while enabling Amazon. And so on. Schumpeter famously described this phenomenon as "creative destruction"; but we can legitimately reframe the process as *creative clearing.* Wiping the slate clean. Launching the chaos that creates unforeseen opportunities at a slant and opens up kairotic situations. Or taking advantage of a bit of the chaos in our own lives.

The ancient Greeks were so enamored of the concept that they began worshipping a god named Kairos who was in charge of opportunity and occasion. (The Romans later called him Occasio.) Youngest son of Zeus, Kairos mated with Tyche, the goddess of fortune, forming a brilliant marriage of timing and luck. The ancient Greeks built an altar to Kairos near the entrance to the sports stadium at Olympus and commissioned the great sculptor Lysippos to create a bronze statue. He portrayed Kairos as a beautiful young man with winged feet who stood on tiptoe as if running a race. While the god's hair grew fashionably long in front, if you walked behind him, you would observe that the back of his head was completely bald. The sculptor was making a point: opportunity ages quickly. To meet Kairos, one contemporary poet wrote, you have to seize him by the forelock before he rushes by. While one literally cannot kill time—Kairos and his Grandfather Time, Kronos, were immortal—you can occasionally catch it. The question is how.

Gap Spotting

Kairos is all about temporary gaps, the void between *is* and *ought,* between rules and freedom (or lawlessness), and between common wisdom and shocking reality. Often, kairotic moments are invisible.

It takes a certain habit of mind to see the gaps and understand the opportunities.

Suppose you want to lose weight. Maybe you support more pounds than you'd like simply because of the chaos in your life—the lack of time to cook, conflicting family mealtimes, a schedule change, or (in my case) a broken leg. A job switch, a fresh relationship, a new home in a neighborhood with sidewalks—all these changes can help you break from weight-gaining habits. But a kairotic approach to weight loss can also entail removing time altogether. Instead of setting a particular target—ten pounds in ten weeks, or size four by Memorial Day—maybe focus on the nutrition and exercise that get you to where your body wants to go. If that means, say, looking good naked a year from now, then you are more likely to have achieved a steady state of weight.

A chaotic moment or crisis can even inspire a new change for the better. That painful New Year's Eve, from the moment I hit the ground, I watched my wife and son spring into action. Dorothy ran into the house, fed the cats, put out the candles, and called our daughter, Dorothy Junior. A rapid response nurse in Washington, D.C., she got other nurses to take over her shifts and made plans to come up north. George, meanwhile, checked my eyes for signs of shock. When Dorothy Senior came back out, George lifted me bodily into the car, and Dorothy drove through freezing rain to the hospital. Several days later, a neighbor built a ramp so that I could scoot outside on a plastic sled. Throughout, an astonishing thing occurred to me: I was happy. The leg hurt, but my daughter made the best miso soup and taught me how to bathe without getting my leg wet. Everyone around me was kinder than I felt I deserved—especially my family. I had been absent for much of the kids' childhoods, working long hours and taking all-too-frequent business trips. And here they were, my grown children, and the friends

I'd ignored for years, showing so much love. And I found myself making a change in attitude: I was luckier than I had realized.

Admittedly, this wasn't the kind of change you see in a self-help book. I didn't lose weight or make more money or gain some new skill. But it changed my relationships. I broke my leg, and it mended my family. The gap opened me up to a new place.

To get better at navigating the gaps, we can think the way the ancient Greeks did, by envisioning the messy parts of life geographically. Unlike us moderns, the ancient Sophists were much more place minded. They pictured ideas as points on a map, *topoi*, a topography of thought. It's where we get our *topic*. Rhetoric students would create architectural maps in their heads, with objects or symbols representing each thought. Instead of memorizing their speeches, orators would choose a path through these symbols. Ideas shared in common were *commonplaces*. And arguments took place in the space between these commonplaces—the areas of disagreement. These in-between spaces of belief were rarely stable. Circumstances change, and so do minds. Beliefs shift, blurring the boundaries between opposing ideas and ideologies. This gap between opinions forms a kairotic opportunity that serves as the place for decision. The Romans called this argument-worthy space a *situs,* or site. We call it a *situation.* It's the white space, a void to be filled to meet the moment.

> Exercise: Think of a particularly chaotic time in your work: when a boss was replaced, the budget got cut, partners began a feud—or maybe just when you found yourself loaded with a slew of tasks that went beyond your job description. Draw a mind map, with you in the middle. Your job is to find a route to a better place— a career change, or a position of leadership, or maybe just

> a new assertiveness. Sketch the problem or source of misery as two or more objects. Your boss can be one such "object," a new task another. Show them pushing against each other or sending hostile beams. Label the forces. Draw a terrain, with the most powerful forces on the highest hills. Label everything. Finally, think of where you would create a path or road that takes you in the direction you most want to go. Label that direction. What you're hoping for is a kind of Brigadoon effect, a path that reveals your destination.

Opportunity often entails luck, but what begins as good luck often turns bad, or vice versa. The princes did not choose to go on holiday to Serendib; they were banished to it. The outcome depends on your decision. It also depends on how you frame the situation. Imagine you walk into a bank and spot a twenty-dollar bill on the floor. Is that an opportunity? It sure seems like one. But an opportunity is different from sheer dumb luck in several respects, the most important being this: *Opportunity requires a decision.*

Should you pick up the bill or not? The choice is easy: You stoop down and find yourself richer. But now what? What do you do with the money? Again, most people would not consider this decision very difficult, especially if others in the lobby are looking on. You hand the bill to a teller, or you hold it up and ask if somebody lost it. Or, if you're the self-indulgent type, you quietly pocket the twenty. We might conclude that the version of you who keeps the money is the luckiest. But Aristotle would say that the temperate or courageous character is the happiest, and that the opportunity to prove your upstanding character counts as the greater luck. After all, won't a self-indulgent jerk just spend it on liquor or junk food?

There's a moral to this example. Chaotic moments—a sudden promotion or a piece of bad news—don't determine your future. Your choices do. At this point, I'm hoping you see chaos as an opportunity to match decisions to your soul. You can start by reframing the moment.

Chaotic Reframing

Aristotle seems to have disliked old people; he said they grow sclerotic from years of suffering life's slings and arrows. They cling to whatever good fortune came to them in the past. Any change in society or the economy threatens them.

This is why many of our greatest inventions have been made by young people. Just look at my generation. Back in the sixties and early seventies, most experts in technology saw a future filled with mainframe computers and terminals—centralized machines run by highly trained engineers. Then two masters of chaos, Bill Gates and Steve Jobs, arrived on the scene. Both college dropouts, they came of age at the tail end of the don't-trust-anyone-over-thirty era, when a president attempted to rob a rival's headquarters, the nation shamefacedly abandoned a useless war, and the "better living through chemistry" promised in countless ads was despoiling our air and water. The old rules failed to make sense. Untrammeled by tradition, Gates and Jobs put computers in individuals' hands. We like to think of people like them as "disruptors," but creative entrepreneurs and inventors tend to arise when the world is already disrupted. While their creations may cause further chaos, that rarely is their purpose. Gates and Jobs merely plunged through the chaotic gap.

These days, Gates—now approaching his seventies—presents himself as an old-fashioned philanthropist. Marc Andreessen, who adopted the Defense Department's invention of the hyperlink to create the first popular web browser, today publishes bitter screeds on how underappreciated technologists are. San Francisco, the chaotic capital of computer innovation, is now so mired in regulations that few new things can get built. Aristotle would not find this surprising in a country where a majority of today's registered voters are fifty and older.

Not to pick on our elders; I happen to be one myself. But we all, young and old, live in an increasingly elderly society. When chaos appears, we have to view it as a space to explore and possibly settle, while resisting our elderly culture's urge to build a wall against it.

In short, we need to reframe ourselves as youthful kairoticists willing to step into the eye of the tornado. Or, somewhat less riskily, we can keep our heads and advance when others panic.

Exigence

In times of greatest stress, we tend to ignore what we actually need. The greater the pain, the faster we go for a pill that will temporarily relieve it instead of looking for a cure that will end it. For instance, consider how your family deals with the inevitable opinionated uncle at Thanksgiving dinner. Some relatives take his bait and argue, while others start clearing the table early. A family political clash can turn to chaos, with loved ones shouting at each other and cranberry sauce landing in a cousin's lap. Well, what's the right thing to do when people disagree?

The answer comes from the art of rhetoric: Think about your goal. What do you want? Even better, what could you get out of the situation? Suppose you're the one hosting Thanksgiving this year. The whole purpose of having this loud bunch over was to strengthen family ties. In which case, you wait for a gap in the shouting and turn to the uncle and say, "Bill, we all love you." Sure, that might seem corny. Be prepared to hear snickers from the kids' table. But regardless of your motive, your declaration of love will suck the air out of Bill's diatribe and restore peace to the table. Having set your goal, you turn a confrontation into a solvable rhetorical problem. The rhetorical term for this problem—the need that your persuasive skills can solve—is *exigence*. Often, when you determine the exigence, it can imply a solution in return. Your exigence is peace? Seek peace. Put in your AirPods, or turn to your table mate and discuss this crazy weather, or stand up and put your arms out in a saintly gesture, saying, "None of us wants to fight right now. Who wants seconds?"

What brings peace to the Thanksgiving table similarly applies to other chaotic gaps in your life. Suppose you lose your job. Your instinct might be to panic, then go online and frantically begin a job search. But it might be more helpful to spend an hour or so on your exigence. What do you really want? Obviously, you need an income. But what else? Do you see a chance to change careers? Is there an opening—not just a job opening but a life opening? Where's the might-as-well, the chance to show Fortune and your soul that you have the courage to move on?

Deliberative Rhetoric

During chaotic times, our language tends to limit itself to the present tense. *OMG, what's happening? Quick, do something! Everything is falling apart! Hide! Run!* Less frequently, we find ourselves using the past tense. *What did we do? Who did this? If only we hadn't . . .*

This is when Aristotle's types of rhetoric can come into play. Present-tense rhetoric dedicates itself to discussing bad versus good. *This is terrible! Bad people are doing this to us!* Past-tense, forensic rhetoric blames others, or ourselves, for ill fortune. Neither kind of rhetoric offers us a way to make good decisions. This is why Aristotle favored **deliberative rhetoric**, which helps us consider the choices we can make. What should we do to get the best outcome?

Sometimes we just need to monitor the tense. *What are we going to do? What if we* . . . Your childcare provider suddenly shuts down just when things are craziest at work. You can spend your time finding out why this happened. You can go online and complain about evil corporations running childcare businesses for profit. Or you can think about how to solve your particular problem. While a brilliant solution to childcare rarely offers itself, maybe this crisis suggests a way to refigure the times you work at home. Or you might reframe your relationship with your retired mother-in-law or rethink your career. You may still lose your head in the land of Serendib, that strange territory of chaos and opportunity. But you just might find fortune. That attitude alone, wondering whether this bit of chaos offers an opening, will benefit you in the long run. When you're hit by another crisis—the landowner raises the rent, or your spouse breaks a leg, or your daughter gets engaged and expects you to pay for a ridiculously expensive wedding—you'll start to think kairotically. Is this a moment to be seized? What's the bigger, more interesting, more meaningful opening?

Nostalgia Cure

Our lives are like Heraclitus's river, a stream that transforms itself through constant flow. You can't step into the same stream twice, Heraclitus said. And it's impossible to return to a life that has already rushed by. The temptation to set the clock back and go home to our past, a home that no longer exists, can debilitate us if we feel it strongly enough. This yearning for home gave rise to the term *nostalgia*. A combination of the Greek words for "homecoming" and "pain," the word was coined by a Swiss medical student in the early 1700s to describe the condition of mercenary soldiers who suffered from sadness and loss of sleep and appetite.

There's nothing wrong with indulging in the happy memories of our youth. Go online and order Blow Pops and Jelly Bellies. Stream old shows. Bore children with detailed descriptions of landlines and 8-track cassettes. But when memory becomes painful, consider yourself in the throes of a disease. A pathological desire for the past stifles any vision for the future and cripples our ability to make a change for the better.

Rhetoric offers two immediate cures. The first comes from Aristotle: Remember the bad times as well as the good. Life is hard and always has been. You are what you are today not just because of the music you blasted or the traditions you followed but because of how you responded to the bad times. A false belief that you can recapture an era—short of a theme party—is a delusion. You can restore your character, but not the time.

Another cure can come from creating things to look forward to. When I was young, the future could not come soon enough. The moon landing seemed to take forever. We were promised computer terminals in our very own homes, but not for many years. Walter Cronkite, America's most trusted newscaster, predicted that cars would someday drive themselves. And even fly! We were too young and too excited for the future to dwell in the past.

Go on, roll your eyes. Think of the threats all you want. But the assumption of an entirely ghastly future constitutes a fallacy. Behaviorists call it pessimism bias, and it lies at the root of depression. Good fortune always accompanies bad. Aristotle noted that we show our characters by our attitudes toward both. But he also said that old people have a harder time viewing the future without dread. One solution is to solve the disease of nostalgia by turning it into a cure. Remember when we were children, and an exciting future of technology and independence seemed achingly far away. That way, change won't just seem impossible. It'll seem downright tantalizing.

Chaos opens up spaces in our lives. When we learn to move through these spaces, boldly going to unexplored territories, we establish agency. Like NASA, only with horrible commutes and small children. Now let's find your destination.

> Exercise: Make a happy plan for a vacation, home improvement, or a new life as a remote-working consultant. Whatever it is, frame it as a return to the future you once loved.

THE TOOLS

<u>Gap spotting.</u> Think of the messy times of life geographically, as temporary openings ripe for decision.

<u>Chaotic reframing.</u> You can fall through a gap or use it as an opening—an opportunity.

<u>Exigence.</u> Examine the exact problem that needs solving. In the midst of chaos, avoid freaking out about the mess. Focus on what you need. Your ability to make the right decision, Aristotle wrote, proves your soul's nobility.

<u>Deliberative rhetoric.</u> This language deals with the future, arguing choices that lead to the best outcomes. The past tense has to do with former sins, crime, and punishment.

The present tense covers values—right and wrong, who's good and who's bad. In a chaotic situation, don't prosecute. Make a decision.

<u>Nostalgia cure.</u> Remember the good times, but don't try to restore them. Instead, think of how much you used to look forward to the future. How can you regain that attitude? One immediate solution: remind yourself that pessimism bias is a fallacy.

3

Inspiration

Find Illumination

Muses, molecules, and other means of great ideas

"As sight is the most highly developed sense, the name *phantasia* [imagination] has been formed from *phaos* [light] because it is not possible to see without light."

—Aristotle, *On the Soul*

Once upon a biblical time—nine o'clock in the morning, according to scripture—Jesus's disciples were sitting around enjoying a tot of breakfast wine. Suddenly they heard a whooshing sound, and tongues of flame shot into some of them. The stricken disciples began speaking languages from around the known world. They were, in short, inspired.

This clearly isn't the most comfortable way to find inspiration. Still, at this point you may have desires but have not yet settled on an interesting goal and can use some creative spark. Or maybe you simply want to become more creative. This chapter can help. Let's start by questioning that word *creative*. Does a selfie in front of an interesting tree count as creative? A new way to accessorize an outfit? A holiday letter with a cool font? Sure. Maybe. But a more hyperbolic approach to creativity might incline toward something mind-blowingly wonderful.

In other words, maybe we don't need creativity so much as we need inspiration. True, the fiery breath of God pushing into the disciples' lungs—a sort of creative CPR—could not have been pleasant. (Those of us seeking inspiration should take care what we wish for.) But once you learn the tools, you might find yourself inspired with a brilliant plan—or, at the least, a more interesting life.

Medieval Aristotelians, being passionate taxonomists, delineated five classes of inspiration:

> <u>Verbal</u> inspiration comes straight from God in a kind of dictation, as with those inflamed disciples. Ghostwriters receive verbal inspiration when they interview their clients. Before you write your own memoirs, you might find this kind of inspiration from writing someone else's. Politicians get verbal inspiration from their speechwriters. Your own memory could arguably provide inspiration. Memorize a speech; when you deliver it, your past self is putting words into your present self's mouth. Of course, none of these projects meets the definition of *inspired* that we're used to. But they can make you seem brilliant.
>
> In <u>plenary</u> inspiration, God's spirit makes every word infallible. Some say that the U.S. Constitution qualifies. Ditto the *Oxford English Dictionary*. Here, the inspiration

comes from absolute trust in the source. In self-persuasion, your soul kicks in. While your own idea to, say, redo a bathroom may not sound altogether original, if you can gin up enough belief in yourself—particularly a faith in your construction chops beyond an impartial evaluation of your real ability—then that self-belief qualifies as inspired.

<u>Moral</u> inspiration moves a person to greater virtue. My wife's best ideas happen to be morally inspired by her love of people. After her father died, Dorothy turned an old flannel sheet into an Advent calendar. She sewed twenty-four pockets, filled each one with a tiny scroll bearing a happy Christmas memory, and gave this inspired gift to her grieving mother.

<u>Mechanical</u> inspiration sparks an action. Think of a gym bro playing heavy metal during a workout. The force of habit could also be seen as a kind of mechanical inspiration. What else is getting us out of bed in the morning?

Finally, there's <u>dynamical</u> inspiration, which literally takes over the recipient's body. Tech gurus say that when general artificial intelligence arrives—"the singularity"—super brains will write their own software and dynamically inspire the robots that will . . . Well, let's not go there.

None of these definitions make it seem likely that you or I will receive bolts of brilliance from above. When humans think of inspiration, we're usually talking about attempting a new idea.

Clearly, we need more help here. Let's look into the concept of ideas.

Think of an Idea as a Molecule

To see how western civilization developed the concept of inspiration, we turn to another *I* word in the *Oxford English Dictionary:* "invention." Our English word comes straight from the Latin *inventio,* meaning, yes, "invention." But the ancients also defined *inventio* as "discovery." Long before the Romans used the word, the ancient Greeks and Jews were coming up with new ideas by finding and using old things in new ways. Aristotle defined rhetoric as the art of applying the "available means" of persuasion. When the biblical Ecclesiastes (the original Hebrew pen name meant "rhetor") wrote "There is nothing new under the sun," he was saying pretty much the same thing as Aristotle.

Our own best ideas tend not to come from thin air. Instead, each idea simply blends at least two ideas. This kind of inspiration is a matter of **compounding**. We combine two elements to make a different thought molecule.

Many of history's greatest inventions are the result of compounding. Economists will tell you that the modern world began in the year 1300 when an accountant in Florence invented double-entry bookkeeping, joining two forms of accounting: income and expenses. Subtract expenses from income and you get zero—another concept, allegedly invented by ancient Arabs.

Or take the iPhone, a complex molecule of existing inventions—GPS, digital camera, microchips, the Internet, streaming services. Steve Jobs's genius was in packaging things that were not so new under the sun.

Exercise: Let's invent things, at least in our heads. Take a notepad and write lists in two columns. In the left column, jot down things you have around the house. In the right column, include things you do every day—certain chores, office work, things with kids, rest, play, or entertainment. Now draw an arrow from one item on the left to one on the right. (Example: rug, exercise. Exercise rug! Bookshelf, entertaining cats. Bookshelves that convert into cat gyms!) You probably won't sell your creations on Etsy, but the exercise should get your juices flowing, preparing you for a genuine combinational inspiration in the future.

Or suppose you have a toddler in the family. She wants desperately to dress herself, which causes chaos when it's time to leave for daycare. List the things she's capable of doing and the things that block her. She can fasten the Velcro on her shoes; she can't button her shirt. Velcro, shirt. You ask a relative to replace the buttons with Velcro. Success!

To Solve a Problem, Refine the Exigence

In the case of inspiration, you want to define the problem as precisely as possible. This is the **exigence**: the exact thing that needs solving. We've already defined *exigence*. Now it's time to drill down and refine it.

Imagine you're a fitness trainer who wants to write a book on equipment-free home workouts. What's your exigence? You might say it's the problem of learning how to write a book. But that thought will not lead to inspiration. You need an idea before you can even think about the problem of creating chapters or finding a literary agent. You go online and learn to your dismay that there already are dozens of books on home workouts without weights—not to mention DVDs and videos and fancy mirrors and the like.

Then one day you pass an elementary school during recess, where first graders are swarming the playground. Some kids tear around, some jump up and down, some stand around arguing, some squat to look at an ant mound, and the rest scramble over the equipment. You spot one little girl in a red sweater. She's doing *all* those things. In intervals. You set the timer on your smartwatch and track her activity—twenty or thirty seconds of frantic bursts, followed by . . . not rest exactly. When she isn't scrambling up the sliding board steps or running to catch up with a friend, she is squatting, or standing with her hip out, or bending over to adjust the Velcro on her shoes.

As a trainer, you know this as active stretching or mobility exercise. The short bursts of activity are "high-intensity cardio sessions." There are plenty of existing workouts that alternate intense activity with short rests. But what interests you are the rest periods. The little girl and most of the other kids on the playground are doing "passive squats"—getting their butts down close to the ground while pulling up a weed or watching a bug. What if you devised an interval workout that devoted the rest periods to flexibility and mobility, making you feel like a kid again? Boom! Inspiration! And then a security guard approaches and you run home dreaming of names for your workout program. Kid Again? The Playground Workout?

Notice what you did to prompt that inspiration. You drilled down to the exigence, the need for a truly original workout. Having done that, you primed yourself to notice things that otherwise might have passed you by. Then you took something that existed—kids playing—and applied it to a different situation: an adult workout.

Playground plus home workout equals... the Kid Again Workout. A good idea? Terrible? Who knows. The point is, you got an idea. An inspiration.

> Exercise: Practice spotting a problem by looking at something needed in your life, or in the lives around you. Then criticize the solutions. The gap between the problem and the cure is the exigence. For example, leaf blowers create a cacophony every fall. The solution, an existing noise ordinance, only covers the hours after dark. People love their leaf blowers, so expanding the noise ordinance would get shouted down. The exigence: making the owners less passionate about their equipment? Incentivizing people to rake their leaves? You may get an idea to sponsor a neighborhood-wide leaf-raking competition.

Call on a Model, or a Prophet

Writers of fiction think like computers, drafting stories with the use of mental algorithms. They create a kind of **model**, just as a computer uses a model to predict the future. Every successful novelist I know tells me that they first come up with a notable character, someone with whom they would love to spend their writing time. The plot arises from the character. The writer pushes the character out of his "before world"—Will Smith finding that Earth is a refugee center for aliens from outer space—and then has that character do what he's most likely to do under those circumstances. This method comes straight out of Aristotle, who said that actions reveal the soul.

Modeling could help inspire your own next great idea, or even an ambitious project.

> Exercise: Write down the first sentence to a story. Invent something of your own or type the first line of an existing short story, novel, or magazine feature. Now put yourself into that scene. What would you do? How would that change things? And how would you respond to the change? You might take this exercise a step further, writing a scene where you embark on some great adventure or acquire an unexpected skill. Exaggerate your courage and your capacity to suffer. Hey, it's only fiction. But what does this reveal about your soul?

Improve an Old Idea

Let's go back to that initium novum, the *Oxford English Dictionary*. The *OED* tells us that an idea forms "an image in the mind." It's something that *occurs* to you, a picture that pops up.

The *OED* also says an idea is a *conception,* implying that your mind gives birth. Here's where the etymology gets interesting: the term *idea* originally appears in Plato's dialogues. His *ideia of the Good* was an ideal form, the true essence of a thing, "an eternally existing pattern or prototype," something pure and unique. That famous cave analogy—the one where the benighted cave prisoners could see only the shadows outside—was all about the *ideia*.

Much of the time, the reality we witness represents only the shadows of the true nature of things. It takes a philosopher (or, in my case, the *OED*) to see the truth behind everything. Michel de Montaigne, a fan of Plato's, decided to drill down to the *ideia* of humanity by studying a single person: himself. His thinking followed a Platonic syllogism:

> *Humans are fundamentally alike.*
> *I am human. Therefore . . .*
> *If I assay himself, I assay humankind.*

It's too late for you and me to invent the essay. But we might come up with something original by borrowing Montaigne's concept of assaying. To assay a mineral is to refine it, melting it down to its original form—its Platonic *ideia*. Our thoughts are like unrefined clumps that we dredged up from our minds. If we write down those thoughts, we can assay them by **refining** them. In our case, this means revision—rewriting and editing.

The writer George Saunders says that revision is a matter of taste. Most of us are better readers than writers. When we read a sentence we have written, we can apply our reading chops to make it better. There's no perfect result. In his book *A Swim in a Pond in the Rain*, Saunders offers a translation exercise using the Russian writer Isaac Babel. He lists five published translations of a single sentence in a Babel short story. Each sentence is significantly different.

> *In verdure-hidden walks wicker chairs gleamed whitely.*

> *Wicker chairs, gleaming white, lined paths overhung with foliage.*

And so on. Saunders writes his own version, and rewrites his rewrite. Each version is great. Which one is the best? That's the point: It's a matter of taste, which comes from you.

What does this have to do with inspiration? Think back to the

Bible's Acts 2, in which the fiery-tongued breath of God comes to some of the apostles, causing each to mouth a different translation of prophecy. Each speaks a different language, *individually*. Inspiration is clearly an individualistic phenomenon. You can wait for it, prompt it, play with combinations of existing ideas, or refine a half-formed idea into a Platonic *ideia* of your intentions. But the inspiration is yours alone.

> Exercise: Have you had a great idea only to learn that someone else came up with it ahead of you? I once thought of retaking the SAT admissions exam and writing about the experience in a magazine. It turned out that several writers had done that ahead of me. So I wrote a paragraph about the idea, just for myself, and then rewrote it, explaining why I had thought about the idea in the first place. My drafts eventually turned into thoughts about exploring my youthful attempts to justify myself. That in turn led to my writing a college essay. I published that experience. You can do the same thing by writing down an existing idea that appeals to you. Keep rewriting it; you may find yourself creating an inspired idea 2.0.

Emerge Phoenix-like from a Failure

While we tend to think of inspiration as bolt-from-the-blue, God-given brilliance, this instant form of ideation tends to be much rarer than the other kinds—plenary, moral, mechanical, and dynamical—that the medieval intellectuals listed. But most often, an opportunity begins as a failure. That's why most of us miss it. George Crum, a chef in New York's Saratoga Springs resort, came up with his greatest invention in response to a grouchy diner. The guest complained that the French fries in Crum's dining room were too thick. Crum, deciding that his French fries currently weren't working, decided to transform them into something else. He shaved the spuds down to a crispy thinness and so, in 1853, invented the potato chip.

Another great failure: Spencer Silver tried to create a stronger adhesive for 3M but ended up making one that was even weaker. One day he spotted a friend using this glue on paper to make bookmarks that would stay on the page. Silver eventually used the discovery to invent the Post-it note.

The history of inventions is full of triumphal screwups, of windows carelessly left open, letting in flies, criminals, scary winds . . . and great creations. While we all have heard ad nauseam about learning from our failures, the examples I gave don't necessarily show a newly acquired wisdom. They resulted in new ideas. Think of your failures as first drafts, and your repeated attempts to make a change as new chances to clarify and improve that first draft. This editorial attitude makes your defeats not just educational but empowering.

> Exercise: This one should seem obvious. Think back on one of your own failures. If you had had your wits about you, what novel solution could you have devised? Could you use that idea next time you screw up?

Create an Opening in Your Mind

When the forked flames descended on the wine drinkers in the New Testament story, the fire entered only some of the disciples. The others must have remained silent or said some version of "Holy cow!" in their native Aramaic. What was it about the foreign-tongued speakers? How were they different from the others? You have to think that these inflamed disciples were somehow more open to inspiration. Maybe the flames actually tried to enter the others, who, being conservative, cautious sorts, understandably blocked their minds against anything foreign.

Picture the disciple who suddenly found himself speaking Persian. Could it be that he let the flame in? In that instant, some part of him said to himself, "Huh. Interesting." Maybe he had a more open soul than his dumbfounded colleagues. This isn't to condemn the uninspired. Our species depends on our more cautious members—the ones who avoid the leaps of faith and survive to pass on their genes. My wife says my last words will probably be "It's doable." Unlike me, she has an admirably conservative—Aristotle would say prudent—soul.

On the other hand, our Persian-speaking disciple helped bring civilization forward. The god of a small tribe of people, restricted to a single language and culture, became universal. The Gospel got translated everywhere.

Michel de Montaigne would say that this disciple was blessed with **liberality**. He believed this to be a form of humility, the kind that's free of the "vanity" of the belief that he is "equal himself to God." Montaigne, that most liberal-minded of souls, opened himself up to foreign ideas without presuming that his culture or beliefs or language was superior to others. He even extended his liberality to other species. How can a person "know the hidden, inward motivations of animate creatures?" he wrote. "When I play with my cat, how do I know that she is not passing time with me rather than I with her?" This inspired sentence reveals a soul that not only suffers the flames to come to him; it allows him to enter the minds of others. No idea would get blocked by this man.

On a more prosaic level, liberality can help suppress the growing doubts in our own beliefs and goals. The great ultramarathon runner Scott Jurek recounts the advice he got from his first coach. "Things will seem like they are going well and you are handling them," Jurek writes. "And then a workout will come that will have you doubting everything. That is when you must truly be open to what it takes to achieve your goals."

How is this related to the inflamed disciples? In our own lives, obstacles and failures shove our plans astray, making them suddenly seem alien to us, separate from our souls. This is when openness, liberality, counts the most. A mistake or failure may seem proof of a wrong direction, or it can be a sign that points you toward serendipity.

THE TOOLS

Compounding. To form an idea, take two or more existing concepts and combine them into a sort of thought molecule. History's greatest inventions come from this kind of prompt.

Modeling. Writers of fiction think like computers, drafting stories with the use of mental algorithms. They create a kind of model, just as a computer uses a model to predict the future. A novelist will conceive a character and then place it in a particular situation—"training" the story. You can do this to write a story of your own future.

Refining. To gain inspiration through refinement, we reshape the lumps of thought that tumble in our heads.

Start with a need and define it as many ways as you can. You may find a solution in that very definition.

Liberality. None of these prompts works unless you first prompt yourself to be open to them. The fiery tongue of inspiration can be scary. We have to be open to our own bizarre ideas, and willing to welcome the strange emanations from alien or divine sources.

4

Hyperbole

Blow Things Up

JFK's lunar trope

"When a man accomplishes something beyond his natural power, or beyond his years, or beyond the measure of people like him, or in a special way . . . his deed will have a high degree of nobleness."

—Aristotle, *Rhetoric*

Even after you have connected with your Aristotelian soul and committed to a goal, you still may not have the means to stay afloat. You need even more motivation. This is understandable. Meeting any ambitious goal entails one big depressing delay in gratification. You starve yourself, exhaust yourself, and beat yourself up. Or you spend frustrating hours practicing a skill in the full knowledge that people have spent lifetimes learning the same thing. (Plus, Malcolm Gladwell's ten-thousand-hours-equals-mastery theory does not hold up in research. Sigh.) This is a terrible paradox. You feel worse in the hope of feeling better.

Diets, workouts, and training plans attempt to deal with this paradox by denying it or employing magical thinking, reversing the pain-to-gain ratio. They demand too little of us while promising unreasonably rapid results.

Fad diets deserve their own low-cal circle of hell, employing fallacious reasoning and tempting gimmickry. They promise dramatic results in record time without regard to what happens a year from now or for the rest of your life. Eat like a caveman, because cavemen looked great in bathing suits! Devour ice cream and lose weight! The most popular diet books work beautifully, given their true purpose: to sell diet books.

More reasonable plans, especially those recommended by doctors, set depressingly low goals. Lose a few pounds and then we'll see. Or walk briskly twenty minutes a day; you may not feel much of a difference, but this is better than nothing.

The problem stems from more than your own moral inertia or lack of time. A failure to improve ourselves may also come from insufficient aspiration. Rather than aiming too high, maybe we expect too little. It's not just that we want to see results immediately; we also find it hard to believe in the promised dramatic results. If a diet claims you'll lose five pounds a day, we think, hey, maybe we'll lose a fraction of that. We set our sights low, try to achieve them immediately, and then suffer the consequences when we fail.

I plead guilty to that behavior myself, having rapidly achieved unimpressive results in woodworking, knitting, Photoshop, music composition, and Esperanto. In each case I succeeded modestly over a short time and ended up forgetting everything I learned—including the reason I wanted to learn it in the first place.

But then I discovered the most glorious trope of all.

Go Fetch

Only a true word geek will understand how a single dictionary entry can turn a person's life around. One day some years ago, I was burdened with work and out of ideas, a bad combination for a writer. Naturally, I sought out every possible distraction. There are few better ways than to look up words in the *Oxford English Dictionary*—in my case, a condensed version in two volumes, with type so small the package includes a magnifying glass. I had bought the dictionary forty years earlier, using all the money earned from bussing tables in my college's dining hall. Looking up a word in those hefty tomes gives its meaning an oracular quality. Go ahead and consult an AI for your etymology; with my *OED* I feel like I'm calling on Calliope, the muse of eloquence.

On this day, I went to the dictionary because of tropes—specifically, the four main rhetorical devices. Why wasn't **hyperbole** usually considered to be one of them? You'll see in chapter nine how those four tropes—metaphor, metonymy, synecdoche, and irony—play pretend with reality. Hyperbole does just that. It blows truth up; or, more rarely, shrinks it down. *Hyper* comes from the Greek, meaning "above" or "beyond." So, what does *bole* mean? I brought the magnifying glass close to the page and . . . eureka! Sheer etymological ecstasy. The Greek *bolē*, the good book says, means "to throw or cast." It's where we get our English *ball*. The ancients, with their unerring poetry, had coined the perfect word: *hyperbole*. To throw beyond. The word just begs us to cast an impossibility into the future and then run after it like a dog playing fetch. "What the hell," I said, smiling, and slid the *OED* back into its slipcase. My day had just gotten way better.

Honestly, "Throw Beyond" sounds like the title to one of those cheesy self-help books. I don't read that kind of thing myself. (Hey, you're not reading one right now, okay? This is *rhetoric*. This is *philosophy*.) Too many self-help books read like fad diets, full of quick and easy solutions that make you worse off in the long run.

And yet, after reading that dictionary entry, I couldn't shake a picture in which I was joyfully throwing myself beyond. The trope was working its synaptic magic. Throw beyond. Go fetch.

Hyperbole has played a remarkable role over the ages, boosting the confidence of athletes, celebrities, entrepreneurs, and Bostonians. A native of that city once read Shakespeare for the first time. "There are not twenty men in Boston who could have written those plays," he said with an admirably hyperbolic air. But while this trope can expand your self-worth, you will see in a bit that it can do much more. If you use it properly, you can set a goal—athletic, intellectual, professional, whatever—that seems just beyond the possible. Then you can use the other rhetorical tools to help achieve it.

The etymology of *hyperbole* comprises more than the biography of a word. The trope's origins can serve as a prophecy, showing us a future of grand, soul-enabled ambition and the hot pursuit of happiness. Yes, this is getting a bit hyperbolic. But with the help of the other tools in this book, you may find yourself elevating your own perceived future to this level.

To be honest, it took me months. But once the trope took over, I found myself transforming from a dabbling dilettante to . . . something more. A Hyperbolist.

A dilettante carries himself a short way and calls it a journey. A Hyperbolist throws beyond and goes on a chase. A dilettante often ends up worse off for having succeeded, eventually putting on more weight than he lost. Or he takes up crocheting for a couple weeks and ends up with a scarf that looks like a triangle. (I speak personally.) A Hyperbolist sets a ridiculously hard goal—say, to crochet the *Mona Lisa*—and, after putting in the time and making nothing that looks like the painting, ends up crafting beautiful scarves.

President Kennedy was speaking hyperbolically when he announced that America would send astronauts to the moon and bring them back within a decade. The technology had not even been invented yet. No one, including Kennedy, knew whether the feat was possible.

> We choose to go to the moon in this decade and do the other things not because they are easy but because they are hard, because that goal will serve to organize and measure the best of our energies and skills, because that challenge is one that we are willing to accept, one we are unwilling to postpone, and one we intend to win, and the others, too.

The speech is rhetorically interesting not just because of the moon but because of the "other things." Kennedy saw the mission as more than a feat of technological prowess or a way to beat the Russians. He knew that the attempt itself would motivate Americans to work for the hard things in general. His address arguably counts as the greatest motivational speech of all time. What's more motivational than a literal moon shot?

A hyperbolic goal can inject moral energy into our own lives, even when the goal itself seems beyond our reach. Years ago, my friend Jim came up with a capital-*H* Hyperbole that entailed hiding canoes beside all the roadless trout ponds he could find in northern New England. He wished to bequeath something of great value to family and friends: a secret map with the location of every canoe. If he tried to accomplish that goal in a couple of months, he would have needed to spend a fortune, buying dozens of new canoes and hiring people to carry the boats to all those places. Plus, he would have had to quit his job to supervise the whole thing. He chose instead to spend his vacations hiking to trout ponds. Meanwhile he scanned local newspapers and websites for used canoes. So far, he has bought and hidden only about half a dozen, carrying them himself. Jim is young and healthy and has the rest of his life to perform his Hyperbole. I have no doubt he'll succeed; this is a guy who, just out of college, built a log cabin on an island by swimming the logs across the lake, one by one. But the goal itself has given his ethos an additional veneer of nobility. Jim is not just a great outdoorsman. He's an outdoorsman with a plan for immortality.

While you may not be ready to conceive your own ideal Hyperbole, it's good to know what qualifies as one:

- It entails some risk, if only of embarrassment. Friends will alarm you with comments like *You're gonna crush this thing, no problem!* Others will text cautionary links.

- It promises something novel and interesting. A bit of quirkiness can help keep friends engaged with the effort.

- It constitutes a first of some sort, making you the original person in a particular category to reach a particular goal.

- As an option, your Hyperbole might climax in a dramatic moment. My own concluded on my birthday.

An ordinary goal is to a Hyperbole what a journey is to an adventure. Instead of trying to overcome a fear of public speaking by simply joining Toastmasters, use the group as a jumping-off point, with the ultimate hyperbolic goal of delivering a viral TEDx Talk. Instead of learning how to cook a decent meal, plan a lavish dinner party for your book club in which you serve "Sylphides à la Crème d'Écrivesses" and "Mignonette de poulet petit Duc" with "Pointes d'asperges à la Mistinguette," along with other dishes made famous by P. G. Wodehouse's fictional chef Anatole.

Or suppose you wish to learn a new language for the sole reason that sophisticated people know more than one. Good luck with that. Far better to think of yourself as a budding cosmopolite who will soon travel abroad and chat up fellow sophisticates. A fine Hyperbole would be to master Esperanto and have fellow speakers welcome you into their homes in Japan and Sweden.

Does all this sound crazy? Will you botch your new language in front of strangers? (I feel you, having once ordered the swimming pool of the day in a French restaurant.) What are the odds that you will get stage fright while delivering a speech on the joys of etymology? Will your Neige aux Perles des Alpes collapse in the oven? It's quite possible. But then that's the very point of a Hyperbole. It should *seem* impossible. As Henry David Thoreau put it, "In the long run men hit only what they aim at."

It's amazing how much better you learn when you're trying to perform the possibly impossible. And what you learn hyperbolically tends to stick.

Achieving the Bald Spot

An even more desperate problem of mine began with a business trip to Dallas. I had gone for a short run after a four-hour flight and then headed into a meeting. When it ended, I stood up and fell flat on my face. My right hip felt as if it had jaywalked into a truck. I couldn't move my leg at all. Colleagues rushed out to buy me a cane so I could hobble to a cab for another meeting. Afterward, I went to the emergency room. "I think I dislocated my hip," I told the doctor.

"Were you in an accident?"

"No, a meeting."

Doctors later diagnosed snapping hip syndrome. My iliotibial band, which runs from knee to hip, was catching against the hip bone on each side. Over the next several years, it cost me sleepless nights and more embarrassing falls. I tried physical therapy, acupuncture, and prescriptions. Nothing worked. I considered surgery, but the surgeon said it would make me even lamer. With enough PT, doctors told me, I might—*might*—be able to go on easy hikes again. Running, hiking, skiing, the sports I loved most, were a thing of the past. It felt as if the story of my life, the tales I liked to tell about myself, had ended. Like the time I hit a deer while cross-country skiing in the dark. Or when I made a tight turn while trail running and pulled a tree down, knocking myself out cold. I'd surprised bears, otters, and moose, and been chased by goshawks. I remembered epic naps on ridgetop lichen, and daylong mountain runs with friends that turned into marathon conversations. Now I had become a character without a story—just some old, broken dude.

"Be grateful," a nurse told me. "You have happy memories."

True, but I also had a disease that wrecks so many men in their fifties: depression, topped with a heavy dose of self-pity. I was on meds for a few years but couldn't quite shake the depression.

Not long after that, I discovered the etymology of *hyperbole*. An idea occurred to me: Recovery would not be my focus. I wouldn't try to get rid of the pain or walk normally or be satisfied with my memories. I would do whatever I could to set back the clock, to not just walk or hike but run, and not just run but run up a particular New Hampshire mountain in quirkily record-breaking fashion. This peak is ideal for testing fitness, requiring a painful combination of leaping power and aerobic capacity. Every fall for many years, the Dartmouth ski team, accompanied by a covey of older athletes, had run up this mountain, timed by coaches armed with stopwatches and two-way radios. When I was in my thirties, I would start last in these time trials, more enthusiast than athlete. The only time I impressed anyone was the morning after a night of drinking with a friend: We killed a bottle of scotch at three A.M., and eight hours later I was running, sort of, in the time trial. I somehow made it to the top, thanks to a hungover persistence that impressed the real runners. This stood as the greatest athletic achievement of my life. Until, possibly, now.

The Abenaki Indians had named the peak Moosilauke, "place that is bald on top." The name suited me; my own top was getting a bit thin. My idea was to become the first person over fifty to "run my age" to the summit, reaching it in fewer minutes than I was years old. Athletes had been using this mountain to test their fitness; the 3.8-mile trail rises 2,800 feet from base to peak, making it the ideal combination of angle and length to measure the body's VO_2 max—its ability to process oxygen. Only a dozen people had run their age up this classic peak, and as far as I could tell, none was over fifty. On the other hand, few geezers had been foolish enough to try. The goal would be impractical, pointless, and stupid, and for the first time in weeks I found myself laughing aloud. I had been overweight and wimpy as a kid; my siblings had called me Fat Baby. Now, in the unlikely event that I ran my age up Mount Moosilauke, I would become, at least in my own mind, a genuine record-breaking athlete.

Even more important, the mountain goal helped me learn ways to train my mind rhetorically. As a writer and editor, I was used to criticizing everything. Nothing was ever good enough; the only thing that made me turn in a manuscript was the deadline—which, being a professional, I stretched past any reasonable definition of *deadline*. My journalism background also made me a skeptic. It was hard to get myself to believe in anything.

Being hypercritical and skeptical will not help when it comes to following through with a Hyperbole. To do the possibly impossible, you must not only believe it possible; you have to see yourself achieving it. Later on, we'll work on the voice in our heads, creating the "charms"—repeated figures—that lead to belief. They not only got me on my feet again; they bent my soul in all the right directions.

To prime your own hyperbolic pump, here are a few examples, corresponding with some common goals.

Lose weight. Schedule a boudoir photo shoot for a year from now. Some photographers specialize in arty shoots where the client—you—appears in a predetermined state of undress. Plan to present a framed photo to your lover while playing music by the British soul band Hot Chocolate. *Where you from, you sexy thing . . .*

Get in shape. While it might seem appealing to look good naked, a more inspiring goal can come from your numerical age. Suppose your fiftieth birthday looms ahead of you, a mere year or so from now. While most people can't do a single push-up, try to make yourself an exception. A Hyperbole would then be fifty push-ups on your fiftieth birthday. Plus, what the heck, fifty pull-ups. And fifty burpees. Or train to do a 10K in under fifty minutes. Extra points if you deign not to share your triumph (or glorious failure) on social media—a feat of modesty that I personally did not attempt. If a chronic health problem puts gym-centric exercises beyond your body's abilities, plan a Hyperbole that seems even more impressive. Get inspired by making a trip to the Boston Marathon on Patriots' Day, the third Monday in April. Cheer on the forty-five racers in the wheelchair division. If you're lucky, Swiss champion Marcel Hug will be competing. Born with spina bifida, he attended a sports school in Switzerland as the only wheelchair athlete. As of this writing he has won Boston six times, and he broke his own record last time around. Beat *that* Hyperbole for joining body and soul.

Learn a new skill. While children who study guitar must suffer recitals as a rite of passage—and guitar schools even inflict that torture on their adult students—you might hyperbolically increase the agony by planning to do some busking, performing on a busy street. Give yourself a couple years of practice, build a set list, and check the local laws. If the thought of playing in front of annoyed strangers does not terrify you, then you have the blood temperature of an alien. Otherwise, use this Hyperbole as incentive to practice all the harder.

A similar Hyperbole can work for learning a language or improving your cooking skills. Plan to give a speech in a foreign country, as a wedding toast or a professional talk (see below). Offer a catered dinner for a charity auction. You don't have to schedule any of these big goals; just give yourself some metrics that let you know when you're ready to commit to the plan. On the other hand, what the heck, make a fool of yourself. Remember, a Hyperbole runs on failure.

Give a speech. Perform an open mic set at a comedy club. Extra points if that thought appalls you. This might be one Hyperbole that can work even—especially—if your Aristotelian soul is more shrinking violet than ham. Give yourself some months to develop a "tight five": five minutes of original jokes. The average open mic set just happens to be twice the length of an average wedding toast. This may make you think that your next wedding toast could offer a kairotic opportunity to try out a comedy routine. But it's probably best to see those two occasions as requiring different expectations of *decorum*—a skill covered in chapter five.

Before you begin writing, binge-watch the series *The Marvelous Mrs. Maisel,* which offers a kind of rolling seminar in standup. Take videos of yourself performing your jokes. And remember, failure is a feature, not a bug. One horrible session in a comedy club will make any other speechmaking seem a breeze. After your first disastrous set, write up a routine about giving a disastrous set at a comedy club. Then congratulate yourself on your amazing chutzpah and settle for giving great wedding toasts.

Improve your love life. Back when I was the editor of a large-circulation magazine, a colleague challenged me to assign myself a story with the largest possible expense account. Our February issue was approaching, and I needed a Valentine-worthy article. So I came up with an idea for a piece titled "Fifty Ways to Woo Your Lover."

Disclosure: I'm not good at romance; I once bought a dozen roses and split them between the two women I was dating, only to have them compare notes. So it seemed funny to try an experiment: I would invite my wife on a romantic trip, on which I would demonstrate fifty proofs of my love over the course of a week. I wouldn't tell her that the trip constituted journalistic research. With the help of a savvy PR person, I booked us into five-star hotels in Florida. We dined at expensive restaurants, strolled on lovely beaches, and shopped in boutiques. In one hotel, I arranged for rose petals to be scattered on a big bed while we sipped Champagne in a hot tub.

In advance of the trip, I thought up and memorized the sweetest, sappiest lines to dole out to my wife. Best of all, the publicist arranged for us to spend the night in a cabin in the middle of the Center for Great Apes, a sanctuary for chimpanzees and orangutans. We fell asleep to nighttime howls, feeling like the original explorers of love.

The experiment had to do with how Dorothy would react to all that wooing. Would she get suspicious, wondering whether I was compensating for something I had done? Would she think I had changed into a middle-aged Romeo? Or was she so deluded as a loving wife that she thought all that romance was normal behavior on my part?

On our last day, as we sat by the water on an island off Miami, I gave her a diamond ring I had paid for personally, and I spilled the beans on my plot. Dorothy said she wasn't surprised by any of my wooing. "You've always been a romantic," she said, showing complete delusion. And then she uttered the most loving thing, her eyes glowing with pride: "Did you expense the ring?"

An even greater Hyperbole for you would be to find fifty "woos" and deploy them in a week, without expensing a single one.

THE TOOL

Hyperbole, the trope that throws beyond. The capital-*H*, aspirational version should entail some novel feat that lies just beyond the realm of the possible—preferably something unprecedented, at least by anyone you know.

It should entail some risk, if only of humiliation. Ideally, it should conclude in a dramatic moment.

Because it requires the full set of self-directed rhetorical tools, a grand Hyperbole can tap into your noblest traits, reset your frame of mind—and possibly bend your very soul.

Part 2

GRASP

5

Ethos

Trust Yourself

Ben Franklin's chastity experiment

"The good man should be a lover of self, for he will both himself profit by doing noble acts, and will benefit his fellows; but the wicked man should not."

—Aristotle, *Nicomachean Ethics*

Why do we fall in love? A dozen roses, diamond rings, dreams for sale and fairy tales? Rhetoric offers a realistic (and more affordable) answer: *ethos,* the impression we have of someone's character. We fall for a person who seems beautiful and kind, fun and smart, the ideal of a human . . . no, a Greek god! As the pop singer and instinctive rhetorician Kelly Clarkson puts it, "My heart keeps callin' and I keep on fallin'." We would do anything to win the affection of this divine being, so we throw ourselves into projecting an ethos that seems worthy of our crush.

This task of winning over a beloved gets much easier when we know the right persuasive techniques. The tools that convey the ideal rhetorical character combine an irresistible mix of beneficence, deftness, and rectitude that perfectly suits the desires of the beloved—or, as we say in rhetoric, the "audience."

Which strategy you employ depends entirely on the audience. You would not display ideal beneficence to a vegan by signing up for the Carnivore Club. A fashion maven would not appreciate your deftness if you showed up wearing sensible shoes. And you most definitely should not pick up a climate activist in a fifty-foot recreational vehicle. The proper "ethical" behavior, projecting a suitable ethos in each separate case, might be a farm-to-table restaurant, Gucci pumps, and a tandem bicycle.

Right, so, what if that audience—the one you need to carry out your heart's desire—is you? How can you give the perfect impression of yourself to yourself?

Thankfully, Aristotle comes to the rescue. Some of the most persuasive motivational devices have to do with rhetorical magnets—tools that attach your audience to you, reducing the gap between your daily self and your soul. The more a person feels attracted, the more she wants to do things for you. You can see this attraction theory in successful dictators. People will literally die for the leader they worship. If the rhetorical techniques of attraction work that well for a murderous despot, imagine how they could help you develop a good morning habit.

Personally, though, my soul and I had a problem. Having come up with my own Hyperbole, I was filled with what those grim psychologists call unrealistic optimism, and wild to get started. "Run my age" up a mountain when I had shown no sign of being an athlete in the previous half century? And when I had not yet gotten rid of a nasty limp? That just made the feat more . . . special. More noble.

But beneath all that healthy delusion lay a quivering bog of doubt. Was I really up to this? Exactly why did I want to do it? And had I strayed too far from my Aristotelian soul ever to close the gap?

The Movie Star Conundrum

Not that you should feel awful if you seem to be straying from your soul's best life. Circumstances can push you off course, at least temporarily. Consider yourself lucky if you can get back on track. You might find inspiration from Hedwig Eva Maria Kiesler. This Austrian-born woman had a lifelong problem with her role in society: She was too beautiful for her soul. Raised in Vienna by her doting banker father, little Hedy had a precocious love of machinery and chemistry. In a different era, she might have trained to become a scientist. But she was simply too lovely, one of the great beauties of her time, and the pull of fame proved too powerful. She was acting in movies at age sixteen and, at eighteen, appeared nude in a scandalous 1933 Czech film titled *Ecstasy*. She met movie mogul Louis B. Mayer in London and followed him to Hollywood, where she became one of the greatest film stars of the golden age. It was Mayer who changed her name to Hedy Lamarr.

Her soul came through in her spare time. She had technical equipment installed in her home, and even in her trailer on movie sets, using these setups to invent things. Her greatest creation was a form of radio-frequency hopping, a technology that would allow radio-controlled British torpedoes to avoid German jamming. The concept eventually led to the creation of aerial drones, Wi-Fi, and Bluetooth. While she acted for money, her passion was science. But when she grew old, her identity as a former Most Beautiful Woman made her withdraw from life, living like a hermit and abandoning her science.

While I'm no Hedy Lamarr in either the looks or the inventions department, when I entered my fifties I realized that my advancing age was also making me more of a hermit. I was feeling the cognitive dissonance between the life that had suited my inner self and the one I had been leading for more than a decade.

But then I thought of Benjamin Franklin. Like Hedy Lamarr, he had the soul of a scientist without the education. Unlike her, he seemed to get along beautifully with his soul. In addition to experimenting with electricity and ocean temperatures, he carried out interesting tests on himself. At the age of twenty-two he set out to prove the hypothesis that he could achieve moral perfection. "I wished to live without committing any fault at any time," he recalled as an old man. Taking a sheet of paper, he listed thirteen virtues, ranging from temperance to humility, and then put down a mark for every day of the week he violated one of them. He wrote wistfully, "I soon found I had undertaken a task of more difficulty than I had imagined." The column for one of the virtues, "Chastity," became covered with the marks of failure. He never did master that one; his son, born out of wedlock, became governor of New Jersey.

"On the whole," said Franklin, "I never arrived at the perfection I had been so ambitious of obtaining." But the experiment itself fulfilled a basic need, aligning him with his soul. He claimed he ended up "a happier man than I otherwise should have been if I had not attempted it." While he wanted to be morally perfect, he was acting the part of a scientist. He went on to play the role so well that people called him Dr. Franklin, though his formal education never went beyond grammar school. Even amid failure, Franklin's role was self-harmonious.

Of course, we're all actors playing various roles in life. The ancients recognized this dual nature. In ancient rhetoric, *actio* meant both action and role-playing. We act by doing—going to the gym, eating McDonald's fries, finishing our homework, or sneaking out of our parents' house for a party. We also act by playing a part or feigning an emotion. Rhetoric requires a good deal of acting. Each role we play projects a character that tries to appeal to a particular audience.

This role-play character, the *ethos,* forms the first step toward persuasion. Aristotle called it the most important appeal of all, even more powerful than logic. If people trust you, they are much more likely to follow your opinion and do what you say.

When your Aristotelian soul is your audience, even the most talented actor can feel intimidated. A person who goes out clubbing despite her soul's desire to be more productive in the early morning might want to leave that annoying soul at home. Small foul, no harm; an occasional break from our truest selves can feel like a vacation. Why else would anyone sing at karaoke night?

In my case, though, it seemed that the gap between the nobly striving outdoorsman (my soul's truest projection) and the bum on the couch (the actual person who was thinking these thoughts) might be so vast that soul and daily self could never reconcile.

I knew that, deep down in my truest self, I could overcome my hip problems and run up that mountain. When I got up from the couch, I found stark, painful evidence to the contrary. But all was not lost; far from it. The whole point of this experiment was to test the tools of rhetoric. And Aristotle had come up with a set of tools specifically designed to close the gap between the persuader (my daily self, in this case) and the audience (my soulful self).

Step One: Fake It Decorously

Our job is to convince our souls that they and our daily selves are not so different. We could do this by living perfectly in sync with our souls' noble standards. Good luck with that, Dr. Franklin. An alternative constitutes our first gap-closing rhetorical skill: **decorum**. This is an aptitude for making the audience think you belong to the same tribe and represent the same values.

We often think that decorum denotes politeness. But the original Latin meant "fitness," as in fitting in with a social environment. If you look the same as your audience, speak the same language, dress appropriately, and show interest in the same things, your audience is likely to consider you one of them. When you eat dinner with a group, you try to match your manners with those of your tablemates. If dinner happens to take place in a culture where people eat with their right hands out of a common bowl, you'd best do the same. Ask for a plate and fork, and your audience of tablemates will view you as a foreigner.

Not all the rhetorical tools mean faking it until you make it, but decorum definitely does. Whenever you begin to lose faith in yourself—in Aristotelian terms, whenever you find a gap widening between your noble inner self and your current disappointing behavior—remember: You just need to play pretend. The less you are like your audience, the more you should use the manipulative tools that make your audience believe you belong. In this case, to belong with your soul.

At the beginning of my own experiment, I walked around as if my limp were a kind of swagger, assuming an exaggerated posture and striding as if warming up for a sprint. Yes, this was silly. People on the street gave me funny looks, and Dorothy kept asking if I was okay. But my fake-athlete gait became a habit. And my self-doubt dropped a degree or two. What's more, my behavior provided a kind of segue into the painful resistance and mobility exercises I needed to do each day. Let me put it another way: To convince myself that I was an athlete, I had to pretend I belonged to my athletic self until I could come up with physical proof.

Surprisingly, this method worked for me. By behaving decorously toward myself—acting as if there was no gap between that brave inner person and my timorous daily self—I reduced the gap between the man I was and the man I wanted to be. Yes, I still had to put in the hard physical effort to achieve my athletic goals, but I was able to get past obstacles that threatened to prevent me from ever getting started.

Step Two: Make Friends with Yourself

In addition to achieving decorum with your soul, you can show it some strategic love. In rhetoric, we call this tactic *eunoia*, or capital-C **Caring**. (The Greek word literally means "good name," but it usually gets the awkward translation of "disinterested good will.") To project a likeable and trustworthy ethos, you give the audience the sense that you have their best interest at heart. The same goes for you and your soul. Its needs are your number one interest. You live to serve, or so you make your soul believe. This gets tricky when you think about all the times you betrayed yourself. You can't blame your higher self if it thinks you've failed to act like a soulmate.

One solution is to follow Aristotle's advice on getting along with friends. Ever the rhetorical taxonomist, the philosopher split friendship into three kinds. The first gets formed out of utility. Think political allies, or business partners, or an arranged royal marriage. You become friends to gain a mutual benefit. Your own relationship with your soul may have a degree of utility; after all, you want it to help you make something of your life. Nothing wrong with that. But utility rarely conveys the impression of Caring. And when that friendship becomes less useful, it often disappears. Not a good thing when you happen to be living together—which you and your soul necessarily are.

A bit higher on the friendship scale is the kind of relationship built from pleasure. Aristotle wrote that we tend to like people who have a ready wit or a pleasant demeanor, even if their characters lack much moral fiber. Scamps can make great bar mates. While you can have a good time with them at a weekend or reunion, you wouldn't want to live with that kind of person. Marriages that originate in pure pleasure tend to end in divorce. This kind of friendship does not lead to harmony with your soul. Pleasure has to do with wants; your soul is all about what you really need.

Aristotle believed that the best friendship is a "perfect" one, where two equals want the best for each other. Well. This part sounds easy. Since your soul happens to be you, then obviously you already achieved equality with yourself. Right? Not usually. Your soul, with all those higher virtues and true needs, can seem to live on a more ethereal plane than your less noble daily self.

Still, you can expect your soul to do its best for you, regardless of your lapses. The ancient Greeks believed that we have an absolute, unswerving obligation to serve our closest friends and relatives. That commitment, called **philos**, had almost the force of law. *Philos* comes into play, literally, in the ancient Greek myth of Clytemnestra. The wife of King Agamemnon, one of the Greek leaders in the Trojan War, Clytemnestra was not a happily married woman. For one thing, the king killed her first husband and forced her hand in marriage. Then he sacrificed their daughter to ensure favorable winds for the invading fleet. *Then* he returned with a captive Trojan princess. Having had enough of this man, Clytemnestra murdered Agamemnon in his bath. Besides committing a mortal sin, she left her son, Orestes, with a dilemma. Should he honor philos with his mother by forgiving her? Or should he fulfill his philos by avenging his father? Orestes chose to kill his mother—another mortal sin. Lose-lose. Aristotle used this unhappy tale to illustrate the difficulty of divided loyalty.

The concept of philos can help you reconcile body and soul. Suppose you put yourself on a diet or join a high-intensity gym so that you can look like Ryan Gosling or Margot Robbie. When you attach your goal to a role model, where's the philos? Who exactly are you trying to please with all that self-torture: your soul, or a stranger you've never met?

To test your philos on yourself, imagine your soul as your best friend—not necessarily your coolest, most fashionably dressed friend. This soul doesn't have a fancy car or a million Instagram followers. It hasn't produced a hit film or written the next great American novel. It's just literally your soulmate. You really should stick by this dear friend, but temptations abound. Your soul wants a less prestigious job that offers you humane hours and intellectual stimulation, but you're drawn to a big-shot tech firm. You'll probably be miserable there, but it will give you bragging rights at your high school reunion. Think how your soul would feel, as if you left it alone at a party while you hung out with the swells. This is a philos crime, an abandonment of your obligation toward your deepest self. That separation can cause great unhappiness.

True philos story: A distant relative of mine, a great student in high school, wanted to attend a small college in New England. Her father pressured her to apply to the more prestigious University of Chicago. She dutifully applied and spent a miserable first year in Chicago, then transferred to a small New England college. Her philos to her father had conflicted with her philos to her soul. This hardly counts as a Greek-level tragedy, but she thrived at the small school.

Step Three: Use the Lapse

Assuming that you and your soul are not at the Agamemnon level of dysfunction, we should find it easier to unify our loyalty. The best way is to frame each screwup as an exception that proves a noble rule. Suppose you decide your soul needs you to lower your cholesterol. You carefully compose a meal plan, cook healthy dishes in advance, and swear off desserts. One evening, just three days into this diet, you find yourself standing in your kitchen with a spoon and an empty carton of ice cream that you apparently have just consumed entirely by your horrible self. Oh, the shame! Health coaches will tell you that a lapse like this tends to ruin diets—not because of the ice cream itself but by making you feel like an utter failure. You ate ice cream in blatant violation of your nutrition plan, which proves your inability to stick to one.

Or does it? You followed the diet for seventy-two hours and then cheated for, what, twenty minutes? You can truthfully tell your sorrowful soul that your discipline-to-cheating ratio is 216 to 1. So far you have achieved a .04 percent error rate. This kind of thinking allows you to practice **sin recovery:**

First, view the mistake as a temporary one that does not in any way prove a sinful nature. One swallow does not make a glutton.

Second, pitch the sin as proof of your deepest values. If you truly were an awful person, then you would not see your action as a sin at all. Instead, the feeling of shame that accompanied your ice cream headache shows how badly you want to live up to your soul's high standards. Now resume your diet, knowing that you probably will sin again. But that lapse will be only temporary, allowing you to maintain an adequately saintly success ratio.

Finally, trust that your soul will forgive you and wants nothing but the best for you. This is what philos is all about. It not only constitutes the best way to sustain a friendship with ourselves; it's the eternal law of the gods.

Step Four: Play Up Your Strengths

We've now paid proper attention to Caring, that trait of a successful ethos that maintains a deep friendship with your soul and lets you believe in the value of the change you want. Now it's time to start believing in your ability to make that change. Here Aristotle's second ethos tool comes into play: *phronesis* ("practical wisdom"). Phronesis gives the impression that you know exactly what to do. I call this quality **Craft**. This is the audience's belief that you can deftly solve the problems at hand. You are not just caring but capable. You have the right combination of experience, street wisdom, and knowledge to solve the problems that your audience faces. I hope you never need to escape from a prison camp, but if you do, a MacGyver-level Craft trait would make your audience believe you can whip up an ultralight airplane from some garbage bags, bamboo, and a generator.

If you want to learn more about a topic or become a better cook, does that mean you have to earn a higher degree or apprentice yourself to a celebrity chef? This is rhetoric, not résumé building. Rhetorical craft is an *impression* of ability. You can achieve that effect through the right manipulative tools. These devices come in handy when you attempt a skill you completely lack.

Suppose you want to learn to play the guitar. How can you convince your soul of your musical prowess without a single lesson? The answer has to do with deeper, more fundamental abilities. If you happen to be a fast learner, then this is all the Craft you need to convince your soul that you will become a great guitar player soon. Or maybe you're a slow learner; still, whatever knowledge you gain tends to stick. Brilliant! You keep what you painstakingly learn. The elements of Craft do not have to apply to the specific skill of guitar playing. Your skill is skills acquisition.

But then, suppose you never were that great a student. Suppose you just happen to be extremely stubborn. Good for you; you never give up! Someday you will bring that instrument to its knees and make it do your bidding. If you can convince your soul that you have one of these powers, then you can motivate yourself to try things that you have not yet mastered. Even in the face of your own doubts, and daily proof of your ineptness, you still have the higher Craft. It will win in the end.

Rhetorical Craft seems to come harder for women than for men in our society. Plenty of research shows that women suffer more from imposter syndrome. Men will say "I could do that" even if they lack the faintest clue. We tend to see proof of our Craft in the scantest bit of evidence. A man who tightens a doorknob qualifies in his mind as a handyman for life. This happy self-delusion gives him the courage and motivation to redo an entire bathroom. True, the result may be appalling; but we're talking motivation here, not tiling. Women, on the other hand, often fail to feel qualified enough. They tend to consider themselves Hermione Grangers—Mudbloods, mere half wizards, imperfect mortals who compensate by studying harder than the men. The answer to this sort of imposter syndrome is not a Y chromosome but a healthy dose of rhetoric. It can help reframe a failure into a signal of your deeper nobility—patience or stubbornness or the knack of learning from your mistakes. And any success truly shows proof of your rising mastery. I especially love this part of rhetoric, because it sets up a bold distinction between pure logic and the kind that builds worlds.

> Exercise: List all your skills, however trivial. Include the ones you worked hardest to obtain. Anything that ends the sentence "I'm good at . . ." counts. Circle the skills that might even remotely apply to something you want to accomplish, such as a new habit or goal. In chapter five, you'll pick up *analogous thinking*—ways to link seemingly unlike things to create belief.

Step Five: Make It a Cause

Having covered Craft and Caring in this chapter, the next obvious step would be to deal with *arete* ("virtue"), or **Cause**, the noblest trait of all. But whether you noticed it or not, we already covered virtue. You have met your soul, which represents your noblest self. Throughout this book, you will discover ways to use your soul to find your final cause. When you do, you can apply your Craft and engage your soul's philos to help meet that Cause.

Elon Musk says his Cause is to save the future of humanity. In your case it might be something less ambitious but, to you, just as interesting. Once you become fully aware of your Cause, you can begin convincing your soul that you live up to its potential. You do this by making a series of choices, and then putting them on autopilot. Aristotle said the choices we make end up revealing our true character. Our relationship with our soul helps us put a spin, some body English, on the ways we make those choices, or avoid making them.

All this is a lot to absorb. You may be asking at this point what you should be saying to your soul, and how to say it without seeming to be off your rocker. All this time we've talked about ways to convince your soul that you have the ideal ethos—wanting only what your soul wants, being capable of any task and dedicated to a higher cause. But *how*? Are you speaking aloud to your higher self? Texting it? Sending telepathic messages while staring in the mirror?

So far, all this may seem like Professor Harold Hill's Think Method in *The Music Man*. Instead of actually teaching kids how to play their instruments—a skill he himself doesn't have—he tells them to think of the music. Well, we are just thinking right now; but we will have to do more than that. We need to persuade our souls and let them persuade us in return. All of this starts by getting in the mood for persuasion.

THE TOOLS

Decorum. This is the skill of making your audience feel that you belong to their tribe; or, in the case of your relation to your soul, that you stand worthy of your noblest self. You share its values and do your best to live up to them.

Caring. One of Aristotle's three qualities of a likeable and trustworthy *ethos*, or character. The audience—your soul—believes that you have only its best interests at heart. Aristotle thought this trait to be the ultimate sign of a "perfect" friendship, where both parties—you and your soul—want only the best for each other.

Philos. The holy obligation among friends or family. It is a soul-centered quality that reminds you that you can depend on your soul to do its best for you. This includes forgiving you when your daily self strays from the path of righteousness.

Sin recovery. For those times when you lapse from your best behavior, admit the sin. Then tell your judgmental soul that it was temporary and that you feel bad about it—a reaction that proves you care deeply about the values you violated.

Craft. The second Aristotelian ethos trait constitutes the ability to make your audience believe you can solve the problems at hand. Craft, like Caring, is rhetorical; a panel of experts may not believe you have the learning and experience to take on a big challenge. But rhetorical craft is a tool you use to play up your strong points—your ability to learn, your great memory, or your perseverance.

Cause. Aristotle saw this tool as the third and most important quality of ethos. His *arete*, or virtue, makes the audience believe you share its values and live up to them. In self-persuasion, Cause links to our essential purpose. The actions we take through life unfold that purpose.

6

Pathos

Control Your Mood

Caesar's hilarious compendium of jokes

"The listener always empathizes with the man who speaks emotively, even if he is talking nonsense."

Aristotle, *Rhetoric*

In Aristotle's wonderfully strange book *On the Soul*, he writes that two factors motivate people: thought and appetite. We'll tackle thought later. Here we deal with appetite. The philosopher meant much more than a growling stomach, though his theory can help explain why diets fail. His "appetite" covers all the emotions, from hunger and envy to fear and confidence, pity and levity.

According to Aristotle, the emotions offer clear ways to get to know our souls. Appetite and its accompanying passions and desires connect the soul to the body. These links provide the most efficient ways to put yourself in the right mood for your persuasion.

When body and soul feel good—calm, well-liked, respected, "and having a good time," as Aristotle put it—we're especially ripe for manipulation.

The problem is, sweating in front of strangers in a gym or struggling through Italian verb tenses rarely count as good times. Any activity that involves discomfort or heavy thinking puts us in the least persuadable state of all. Hard thought burns a great deal of energy, and our species has evolved to spend as little time as possible doing it. When something goes wrong with my wife's laptop, she stares at the thing with a deep frown and, uncharacteristically, talks like a sailor. The worst thing I could say to her at that moment would be a sentence beginning with "Maybe you should try . . ." Her brain is walled off from any outside influence.

Next time you find yourself bingeing on Netflix instead of studying something useful, just know that your thought-avoiding behavior evolved as a matter of survival. I like to think that the Neanderthals were especially thoughtful sorts who burned so much mental energy that they all starved themselves out of existence. Meanwhile, our boneheaded forebears efficiently limited their thinking to mammoth hunting and the avoidance of tigers. Given our heredity, it's easy to see why it can be so hard to accomplish anything difficult, or to learn something that lies far outside our expertise. While motivating ourselves requires self-persuasion, the very effort of persuading ourselves into self-motivation makes us resistant to persuasion, including our own. A vicious exercycle, if you will.

This chapter will help you overcome that dilemma by taking an Aristotelian approach to your feelings. You will find ancient ways to bend your mood and make yourself more open to self-persuasion, even during the most agonizing, why-am-I-doing-this bout of striving.

Modern researchers have studied the emotion of persuadability, or **cognitive ease:** that sweetly thoughtless emotional condition that makes an audience easy to manipulate. While Aristotle calls it "receptivity," I describe it as the Homer Simpson state. The cognitively easy audience feels happy, smiley, carefree, and most of all, empowered. (As dear Homer himself put it, "All I want is what everybody wants: preferential treatment.") This state allows people to get together and join forces behind a compelling, persuasive leader—which, in this case, is your soul-bending self.

Let's run through an Aristotelian taxonomy of emotions and find the cognitively easiest ones, to match your goals.

Confidence: Be the Billionaire

Aristotle's version of confidence comes from a sense of power. People who feel themselves to be in the lead are, ironically, easier to manipulate. Psychologists say that if you want to sell something, you should put yourself in a seat below that of your client. Over the long term, the feeling of power comes from the audience believing it is strong, rich, and popular; and, Aristotle adds, well armed.

Let's stick to strong, rich, and popular.

This is a deeply rhetorical concept. The ancients believed that *pathos,* or emotion, comes from the mind's interpretation of experiences. What happens to you gets filtered through your mind as an imagined version of reality. This takes us back to Plato's cave. His Socrates claims that we see only the shadows of what is real, and we think this is reality. Plato, who claimed to despise rhetoric, wanted us to see beyond the cave of our minds and understand what is real. But is strength absolute? Is money "real"? Exactly how many friends do you need to be officially popular? Much of what we call reality—the Sophist Gorgias would say all of it—is a matter of interpretation, and our perception of our own awesomeness lies behind the feeling of confidence.

Pretty philosophical stuff, I know. Let's apply this concept, using a practical example: overcoming a fear of public speaking. Many years ago, I was scheduled to give a big presentation in front of the top brass of an airline. I was feeling more than just jitters; my mood was full-on imposter syndrome. My audience comprised masters of the universe, with business degrees and responsibility for hundreds of airplanes and millions of passengers. They wore expensive suits and could command the rapt attention of thousands of stakeholders and analysts. I was . . . a *citizen* of the universe, with a liberal arts degree and a staff of six. I wasn't rich or strong. My popularity was limited to my family, a few friends, and a cat (though I wasn't so sure about the cat).

My mental preparation might seem silly to anyone who hasn't read Aristotle. First, I went into one of Manhattan's fanciest buildings and bought myself a watch for a breathtaking ninety dollars. (It was years ago, remember. And "expensive" is relative.) Next, I played up in my head the drama of appearing alone in front of a C-suite of powerful men. (Yeah, years ago. All men.) Finally, I remembered a trick from junior high, when I had been an unpopular seventh grader. Before entering any classroom at school, I determined to smile as if I had just heard a funny joke from a good pal. This probably made zero impression on my classmates, but it did wonders for my own self-impression. Some part of me—call it my Aristotelian soul—began to believe that I was pretty darn popular. So, enriched by my ninety-dollar watch and impressed with my own bravery, I was ushered into the airline's high-floor conference room, smiling as if some executive had just told some inside joke. My grin probably did nothing to impress my audience. But I felt rich, powerful, and popular enough. The meeting went well.

Since then, I've used this confidence trifecta whenever I've felt nervous. My fundraiser wife often brings me to dinner parties with extremely wealthy people, where I feel like a peasant at the palace. As our car winds its way up the inevitably long drive, I make myself feel the equal of these fancy people by reframing wealth as education. After all, I have read Aristotle. Have they read Aristotle? As for power, I call on all my strengths: the table manners my mother taught me, the rhetorical skills Aristotle and the others taught me, and . . . did I tell you I read Aristotle?

> Exercise: What would you do differently if you had a billion dollars? Now ask yourself whether you could do pretty much the same things without the billion. Benjamin Franklin believed that wealth meant independence, the ability to live your best life. Or, as Kris Kristofferson put it, "Freedom's just another word for nothing left to lose." Which is as good as wealth if you spin it right. What you're really doing here is reframing wealth in terms of Aristotle's other sources of power: strength and popularity.

Shame: Be the Zipper

Shame tends to be a public thing—the embarrassment you feel in front of one or more appalled onlookers. In describing the emotion, Aristotle referred to an ancient proverb about "shame dwelling in the eyes." He meant that this emotion requires an audience. The more beloved, feared, or respected the audience, the worse the shame.

When you feel ashamed of yourself, your audience is your own disappointed soul. We call a person who is utterly without shame "soulless." Vampires are notoriously without shame; when they look in the mirror, they see only the mirror. They can't see their soul, because they *have* no soul.

Shame comes from acting ignobly—without virtue—violating the standards of your audience. I felt memorable shame when, soon after college, I began working in an office one floor above an attractive young woman. I was bantering with her in a hallway, displaying what I thought to be my debonair wit, when she pointed at my crotch and said, "Your fly is down." I literally sank to the floor with my hands modestly crossed. She later told me she found this more charming than my conversation. Aristotle might say she admired my soul's instant reaction to my active self's cluelessness. Four years later, the woman married me.

Note that while I experienced shame, my absentmindedness didn't make me feel guilty. Shame is not guilt. While they are close cousins, they're not identical. Guilt is a form of long-term punishment for past sins. Shame comes and goes; you zip up your pants and get on with life. While guilt may require therapy to relieve, shame is temporary. And that, in a way, makes it a positive emotion. For one thing, shame may be the single easiest way to detect your soul. If you feel shame for doing something when you're entirely alone, then you are receiving a signal from that temporarily disenchanted companion. Just listen to the good sense emanating from your soul. Shame is the feeling of that good sense.

Fear: The Secret Is Timing

Terror turns people instantly obedient. Yell "Duck!" on a crowded sidewalk and watch people crouch. Yell "Fire!" in a theater and . . .

the Supreme Court specifically excluded that from the protections of the First Amendment, for the obvious reason that panic can cause a stampede.

In fact, the immediacy of panic creates a problem for useful persuasion. Aristotle defined fear as "a kind of pain or disturbance resulting from the imagination of impending danger, either destructive or harmful." Impending danger blocks any thinking about the future except for immediate avoidance. When someone yells, "Hit the deck," you hit the deck. You don't think about staining your pants and the resulting dry-cleaning bills. Fear also blocks all ambition. You want to protect yourself; you don't think about improving yourself.

Aristotle also pointed out that fear is a temporary emotion, which makes it a bad long-term motivator. Suppose you have the terrible feeling that you may not fit into your best outfit in time for a cousin's wedding. That might motivate you temporarily, but fear alone won't do the trick. The emotion never lasts long enough to make an effective change.

But there's an upside to fear's ephemeral nature. If fear comes from "the imagination of impending danger," then your imagination can turn it off as well. Remember when you first learned to drive, and how scary it seemed to be behind the wheel of a two-ton death machine? And how driving on the interstate for the first time made you taste your own heart? You got used to it after a while. While you probably know ways to calm yourself—breathing, relaxing your shoulders, taking a bath—when it comes to talking yourself into accomplishing something difficult, dealing with fear is more a matter of patience. Fear rarely lasts.

> Exercise: If you want, skip ahead to the next chapter to see Aristotle's theory of causes. It will allow you to apply

inductive reasoning to a fear: Is it real? What's the origin? Why does it exist? And does it come from one horrible event, or a pattern? By analyzing your phobia—fear of public speaking, or of heights, or of failure—you just might tamp down the pathos.

Envy: The Most Underrated Sin

In 1987, *Harper's Magazine* asked seven top advertising agencies to devise ads, each promoting a deadly sin. In a fit of self-awareness, every agency complied.

"Lust: Where Would We Be Without It?"

"Pride: The Sin You Can Feel Good About."

"If the Original Sin Had Been Sloth, We'd Still Be in Paradise."

One agency even had Santa Claus endorse greed.
The layouts all looked slick with great photos . . . except for envy. That ad consisted of typewriting on yellow lined paper complaining about how the other agencies got all the fun sins. "Why, they practically sell themselves," the ad griped.
But envy may win in the end. "I rather think that the emotion of jealousy is by far the fiercest of all," Marcus Tullius Cicero wrote. Being the orator he was, Cicero saw envy as a means of arousing the passion of an audience.
One of the biggest problems we face when we try to accomplish something is a growing awareness of people who have already accomplished more than we possibly could. I feel this acutely as a

writer. Every time I read a wonderfully written book, I say to myself, "I'm not worthy." Imagine yourself as a budding standup comedian watching a Netflix special with Chris Rock. Or suppose you happen to be single and looking for love, and you meet a blissfully married couple. This is when you need to slather yourself in the most manipulative rhetoric. Instead of judging yourself, judge them. Think of how unfair life is, and how much nobler you are for starting at the back of the pack.

Aristotle saw envy as a motivator rather than as a sin. "Men are ambitious before competitors and rivals," he said. Could you see your own soul as a rival? Personally, I can't. But sometimes I do resent that sanctimonious do-gooder and overachiever. There are times when I think, "I'll show him!" I'll prove myself to be better than my soul thinks.

Laughter: Be the Fall Guy

Our souls can be intimidating, and we won't always enjoy their perfection; but just as laughter can soften the bumps of a marriage or relationship, a good sense of humor can help us get along with our Aristotelian better halves.

The right kind of laughter, self-persuasively speaking, is gentle self-deprecating humor. It allows that virtual audience inside you to forgive your small venal sins of commission and omission. Laughter can be scornful or relieving; that's up to you and your soul. Meanwhile, unless you happen to be a professional comedian, there's no sense in trying too hard. Constructed humor rarely works. Budding speakers should not tell jokes unless they're sure of the reception. Julius Caesar, who had a reputation for humor, once read a Greek jokes manual titled *Concerning the Laughable*. The advice was so stupid, he said, that the book was unintentionally funny.

Democritus, the ancient Greek who inspired Epicurean philosophy, was known as "the laughing philosopher." He had a sense of the big picture—big as in cosmic. It will take the rest of this book to show what this means. Meanwhile, think of self-deprecating humor as a way of avoiding being intimidated by your oh-so-noble soul.

Desire: Don't Trip Over the Donut

To persuade anyone to take an action, you need to spark a passion, making the audience lust after the result you want. Our appetites can move us to do positive things. But Aristotle pointed out that our desires can conflict. We have many wants; some lead to good ends, some to regrets. The regrettable ones tend to sit on a plate right before us. As Aristotle put it, "Desire is influenced by what is at hand." A donut in front of our nose stimulates action much faster than our desire to have low triglycerides. An invitation to a party can beat the aspiration to study for a four-year degree.

What's more, an immediate temptation precludes thought. See donut, take donut. Conversely, the motivation for actions toward longer-range goals—Aristotle called this "local movement"—requires practical thought to work out a strategy. Suppose you want to change careers. Before you can get yourself to start on a plan, you must hunger for that new career. "For that which is the object of appetite is the stimulant of practical thought," Aristotle wrote. This implies that you can use temptation to your advantage, through a sort of **desire reversal**.

> Exercise: Turn a long-term desire into an immediate one. Focus on the object of your goal. Instead of thinking of studying for a nursing degree, imagine a scenario

where you heroically save a child's life. Turn your eyes from a donut and visualize seeing the soul-satisfying body in the mirror. Your best bet to avoid temptation is to focus on the soul's great goals, rather than your immediate appetite. Make the long-term seem as close as a pastry. No, it's not easy, especially if you can smell the pastry.

Charm: Get That Sweet Placebo Effect

Having run through the range of rhetorically relevant feelings, it's time to deal with the most magical emotion of all: charm. Plato rightly saw charm as a healing strategy as well as an emotion. In one of his dialogues, a young man complains of a terrible headache. Socrates offers a remedy he picked up from a physician in Thrace. Don't worry about the body, he says. Cure the soul, and the headache will go away.

The man asks, How do you cure the soul?

With a "charm," Socrates says, quoting the doctor.

What kind of charm?

"Sweet words."

Just what those sweet words were, Plato leaves out of the dialogue. Socrates might have done better to prescribe willow bark. Still, you can see the positive effects of rhetoric in the placebo effect, the healing that comes from a belief that the cure will work. The pharmaceutical industry spends billions trying to remove the placebo effect from data on their prospective drugs in order to determine their "true" efficacy. But in a rhetorical sense, the placebo effect itself is real. It's based on belief, which in turn can come from sweet words—charms.

Aristotle took the concept further, asserting that you could make yourself *into* a charm. He called this ability *karisma*—a knack for making yourself irresistibly attractive to others. Karisma also alleviates doubt about actions and results, or procedures and cures. A confident-looking doctor in a white coat, standing in front of her impressive degrees, has a medical charm—or, to use a modern spelling, charisma. The charismatic person has an awesome ethos. She shows great Caring, dedicating herself to the concern of others. Her charisma also comes from being successful, a sign of Craft. The more difficult the tasks achieved, the greater the charm.

One of the best examples of success-sourced charm was Robert Moses, the man who built many of the parks and highways in New York and Long Island. A perfectly horrible person in many respects, Moses fought mass transit, destroyed whole neighborhoods, forced lower-class families from their homes, and in general acted like a tyrant. But people loved him for working without a salary (a sign of disinterest, or Caring) and they loved him even more for his Craft—his ability to build things in a city that had been infamous for its infrastructural incompetence. For decades, he was a saint to most New Yorkers. He had the charisma of accomplishment.

What about the rest of us? Suppose you lack a Moses-level résumé. Once again, Aristotle comes to the rescue. He noted that charisma can also come from proving that you suffer well. My friend Dan, a passionate outdoorsman, once led a group of Boy Scouts on a winter hike up one of the highest peaks in New Hampshire. While the boys brought snowshoes, Dan carried skis. After summiting, they began heading back down when Dan slipped and broke his leg. Pushing away the scouts, who were thrilled at the chance to apply first aid, he sent them ahead and then skied down alone on one ski. It wasn't just the skill that made him a charismatic legend among fellow outdoorspeople. It was how well he suffered the pain and effort. People would follow him anywhere into the dangerous wilderness.

To achieve Dan-level charm, remember that suffering can count as a skill. Charm yourself by remembering how much you have proven you can bear misfortune. But, hey, when you break your leg? Get to a hospital. Dan is charismatic, but he's also a little crazy.

> Exercise: Rewrite your résumé emphasizing your accomplishments. What would you consider to be your charms? Those sweet words will boost your confidence as well as your charisma.

Catharsis: The Adele Cure

Each of the emotions has to do with our beliefs, perceptions, and expectations. While Plato thought we should keep from feeling emotions at all, Aristotle was more practical. Emotions are natural. There is no sense in fighting our passions. Instead, we should use them to help bend our souls.

Aristotle wrote that the ability to deal with emotions, "with the right reason and in the right way . . . is the character of virtue." Take fear, for instance. As an ad copywriter might say, where would we be without it? People die from a lack of fear; ask a park ranger in Yellowstone National Park how many fearless people get gored while taking bison selfies (two or three a year in that park alone). On the other hand, we know how much excessive fear can block us. Aristotle taught that the virtuous soul steers us to the middle, halfway between foolhardiness and cowardice. The ideal Greek soldier would duck from incoming spears but wouldn't run away. Aristotle believed we should rule ourselves from the middle—*mediocracy,* he called it, meaning that as a good thing. All our emotions should be in mediocre balance: fear and confidence, shame and envy, pity and humor.

The ancients were all about balance, both in body and mind, and even with the universe. The four elements—earth, fire, water, air—existed in the body as "humors": black bile, blood, phlegm, and yellow bile. When they were out of balance, a doctor would "rectify" them by various methods. He would bleed a feverish patient, since blood represents the fiery element. He would also use cupping, applying a hot glass cup to raise a blister and draw out the offending element.

Few people were born blessed with balanced humors. For the rest of us, the excessive element would have the most influence on both body and soul. A "sanguine" person had a large supply of blood, and this made him an active extrovert. Think Bill Clinton. A watery, phlegmatic personality was the opposite—introverted and cautious. Think Calvin Coolidge. The bad air from too much yellow bile (Darth Vader) would give a person anger issues. Earthy black bile, which the Greeks called *melaena khole,* made a person melancholic (think Hamlet, though he also had his reasons). The act of rebalancing these humors can give you great pleasure, the same feeling you get when you stop running.

One method that Aristotle and his contemporaries proposed for balancing our mood, especially pity and fear, was catharsis, a kind of emotional purification. Tragic plays are a great source of catharsis, he believed. You watch the hero suffer and you walk out of the theater somehow feeling better. If this seems odd, think what a good heartbreak song can do for the soul. Adele has cured melancholy in countless fans. The lovelorn can listen to "Hello" on repeat for a while, cry, then feel much less lorn. What that poor sap feels is what Aristotle called "cathartic pleasure."

That pleasure can get scarce as the years go by. The older we get, the more our characters tend to veer toward the choleric (based on yellow bile). Old people are "sour tempered," Aristotle wrote. Their own past experiences make them fear the future, because "most of the things that happen are bad," he said; "for most things turn out for the worse." Aristotle himself was clearly feeling his age when he wrote that.

In the next chapter, his logic will help us prepare for our future, and even look forward to it.

THE TOOLS

Confidence. Aristotle noted that confidence comes from a perception of wealth, strength, and popularity. Find wealth in whatever independence you have. Interpret your strength in the most positive way. And focus on why your loved ones adore you.

Shame. That admonitory voice in the back of your head is coming from your soul. Use it to detect your better self.

Fear. Distinguish between an immediate threat and a distant danger. A branch breaking overhead triggers a survival response. When you get that same feeling from a scary change, let your rational side take over.

Envy. Turn envy into a desire to achieve. While you're at it, allow yourself to feel envy for your own annoyingly awesome soul. Then set out to prove you're just as good.

Humor. This tool may seem to counteract all the ego-building other devices. But gentle self-deprecating humor can help you get your ego out of the way when it blocks you from your soul's truest needs. Allow yourself to laugh at yourself. This could be a sign of your soul forgiving you.

<u>Desire reversal</u>. Turn distant goals into immediate wants. This takes some imagination. If you want some hints, turn to chapter eleven on creating your own story.

<u>Charm</u>. The best of all pathos tools, charm—charisma—is a belief in your own magic. If this seems impossible at this point, hang on. You'll soon pick up a group of verbal "charms" that work proper magic on your skeptical self.

<u>Catharsis.</u> A way of cleaning the emotional pipes by empathizing with someone pitiable. The blues were invented for this.

7

Logos

Come to Believe

Taylor Swift's rational color

"For all these topics, by defining and fastening the *what-it-is*, lead to deductions about the objects of discourse."

—Aristotle, *Rhetoric*

You've met your Aristotelian soul, contemplated some goals, adjusted your mood, and found ways to join your daily self with that high-hat inner self of yours. In this chapter, we will cover ways to make the impossible seem possible. This gets done through Aristotle's marvelous *logos*, a toolset of . . . well, not logic, exactly. The Greek word covers all kinds of thought, including tricky strategies that play on our more irrational instincts. In rhetoric, you can be cheerfully illogical so long as your persuasion succeeds. But before we can understand the manipulative side of logos, we should get familiar with logic, both pure and rhetorical.

We tend to think of pure logic as an inhuman phenomenon. Artificial intelligence can run algorithms around us. But while Aristotle might marvel at our robots and self-driving cars, he would argue that rhetorical logos is a uniquely human skill.

We use logic to make choices, through deliberative rhetoric. Deliberation lets us decide what paths to take in life. The proper subjects of this kind of rhetoric, Aristotle said, "are naturally traced back to us." In other words, deliberation ignores dumb luck or bitter misfortune. Those things happen, and there's nothing we can do about them. If Aristotle ever played blackjack, it would be hard to imagine him clutching his curly hair over a so-so hand. Instead of decrying the Fates, he would add up the cards, calculate the odds, and decide whether to ask the dealer to hit him with another card.

Of course, a decent AI model could make that calculation for him. But Aristotle would choose whether to use the computer in the first place. That decision would be naturally traced back to him. He might decide that his capacious brain can do the math. Either way, he knows that counting cards merely increases his odds. He could still lose. The Fates alone would be responsible for the outcome.

The Fates have the same power over the past, right up to the moment before this one. The past lies outside our deliberative domain. While we can do something about the life we inherited from our forebears or our own experiences and mistakes, our focus must be on the choices before us, not on what happened already.

Consider the polar bears, those poor carnivorous creatures. While you might not want to meet one intimately in the wild, it's troubling to see them swimming around in an open sea. What will happen to the little cubs who evolved to live on a much icier pole? The Arctic is warming because previous generations pumped massive doses of carbon dioxide into the atmosphere while bequeathing to us an unprecedentedly comfortable lifestyle. We humans have inherited that lifestyle, along with a warming planet. Should we mire ourselves in species-centric guilt? Blame our forebears? Feel terrible about being citizens of a developed country?

Absolutely we can. But these are choices. No one forces us into these emotions. More importantly, the air was getting pumped with CO_2 before we were born. As Aristotle would say, the problem isn't naturally traced to us. If we focus only on how destructive we humans have been to the planet, we feel helpless. While the glaciers melt, we remain frozen.

Aristotle's logic helps to unfreeze us. A young woman concerned about the planet could choose to ride a bike to work, earn an engineering degree and build climate-resilient structures, join the Green Party, or move farther north . . . all these are useful choices. Nothing can be done about the past except to learn from it.

The same thing goes for you and me; what we have inherited, the choices made by our past selves, our institutions and laws and environment: All have been baked into our lives already. Still, we can respond to our outrageous fortune by making choices that just might turn the slings and arrows to our advantage. As the Puritans liked to say, we can "improve our opportunities."

But how do we make those choices—particularly the sorts of decisions that won't make us fear for our souls? We need Aristotle's logic, and a big dose of rhetoric.

Our view of reality—at least the logical part of it—comes from three sources, according to Aristotle:

- Facts

- Beliefs

- Definitions

Let's start with facts and beliefs. They anchor the two kinds of Aristotelian logic, **induction** and **deduction**. We tend to get confused about these two, in large part because of Sherlock Holmes. That silly detective bragged about his deductive powers, when most of his sleuthing had to do with *induction*. Why does it matter whether your logic is inductive or deductive? Because the tools we will use to bend our souls toward our goals depend on using the right one for the right occasion.

Still, if you're anything like me, formal logic has always confused you a little bit. Let's turn that confusion into healthy self-manipulation.

Induction: Detect the Cause

Inductive logic deals with the facts and how you interpret them. Imagine taking a hike with a friend in the New Mexican desert near Area 51. The two of you spot a basketball-sized object partially embedded in the sandy gravel.

"What is it?" your friend asks.

You approach with trepidation. Most of this region is controlled by the air force, whose stray objects tend to explode. But as you get closer, this thing begins to seem weirdly transparent. What bomb would be see-through?

It's time for Aristotle. His version of the scientific method—a system of observation that still gets taught in science and philosophy classes today—breaks down any unidentified object into four "causes."

"What's that thing made of?" you ask. Good job. You're determining the object's *material* cause. Is this mysterious thing made from some kind of plastic? Or . . .

"Whoa, it moved!" You both stare: the thing is . . . undulating! This implies that the material is organic.

"Who do you think made it?" your friend asks. The two of you stare at each other, wondering who will say it first. "Aliens?" You're trying to work out the *efficient* cause, which has to do with the producer of an object.

"Maybe it's some kind of half-living computer brain," says your friend, who reads science fiction. He is talking about the *formal* cause—the form a thing takes. In this case, the form might be that of a brain.

Now your friend moves on to the *final* cause. Feeling more confident about his theory, he says, "I bet it was the brain of an alien spaceship, controlling all its navigation and functions and everything."

While your friend might be entirely wrong—the object could just be some toy that blew in the wind—this logical process is the single best way to examine the strange and mysterious, from interstellar objects to your own unexplored soul.

Let's leave alien brains and examine your own final cause. Like Billie Eilish, you might be asking, "What was I made for?" We're not necessarily talking about your calling or vocation, the purpose for which you were put on the planet. That might be an aspect of your final cause; but when it comes to the final cause of a person, Aristotle would say that it has to do with the ultimate expression of personhood. He's talking about your best life. At the very center of that best life lies your soul, which is at the heart of the changes you most want to make.

Meanwhile, you can use inductive reasoning to see reality more clearly. Imagine yourself to be Taylor Swift, you lucky thing. You are planning your next big concert tour. (I mean, seriously. This would make a decent role-playing game.) You decide that the next big theme will revolve around a color. In fact, why not first record an album around a particular hue? Being the marketing genius you are, you research the trends. What color does your core audience—twelve- to-twenty-five-year-old females—tend to favor most? You, Taylor, follow Aristotle's four inductive steps.

First you ask: *Is it real?* Do girls and young women actually prefer a particular color? You get your people on it, contacting the Pantone color folks and maybe holding some focus groups.

Next, *what's the origin?* Who or what determines whether a seventh-grade fashionista's new backpack is Barbie pink or pansy purple? Who are the color influencers on TikTok? Or are the trends mostly manufactured by the backpack designers? Knowing this can help Taylor anticipate next year's hot color.

Third, *why?* What's the reason for pink versus purple? Does it have to do with the national mood? The rebirth of Barbie? Just what force drives color preferences? What influences the influencers?

Finally, *is this a trend?* Is pink on the rise, or has it peaked and gone past its sell-by date?

This color-trend finding follows Aristotle's inductive "causes"—*material* (is it real?), *efficient* (what's the origin?), *formal* (what's the reason, or what can we honestly call this thing?), and *final* (does this thing have a life of its own?).

Whether or not Taylor Swift ranks among your top passions, the tool of induction can improve your mood. For instance, our digital news feeds constantly bring us horrors from elsewhere: crime, wars, criminal leaders, lions and tigers and bears in trouble: Oh my! Now apply inductive reasoning to each piece of news, and you may find yourself responding differently.

Your smartphone reports that a young child has been kidnapped somewhere in the Midwest. First you ask: *Is the news real,* or is it just rumor—or downright fake? You can investigate further, or you can dismiss the item altogether. Your choice.

Next, *what's the origin*? Did the news come from a source you trust, one that checks its facts and admits its errors?

Third, *why* did the kid get allegedly napped, and by whom? Was it a divorcing parent? A stranger?

Finally, and most important, *what's the trend*? Are kidnappings increasing? Is the number growing nationwide, or just in that one part of the country?

Assuming you care to do the research and cogitation, you might conclude that this terrible event is a single data point and not evidence of a wave of kidnappings. In fact, you may learn that the trend has been going down for decades. You discover that in most cases, we see a very sad story about feuding parents, with the unfortunate child in the middle. Tragic. But not a sign of the apocalypse.

Inductive logic can even help you overcome imposter syndrome, that terribly common ethos ailment. Suppose you have started a new job. *What* exactly is the part of your work that makes you feel unqualified? What *caused* that feeling; the fact that you haven't done this specific work before? A lack of education? Or new colleagues who seem more proficient? *Why* does this seem so important? Is it reasonable to feel that your inadequacy will last *forever*?

Induction might let you avoid imposter syndrome altogether, by allowing you to make more logical decisions. In any major life choice we make, we accumulate facts and reach a conclusion. Before we buy a house, it helps to gather facts about housing trends and mortgage rates and crime and schools, and then draw a mental picture of our place in that reality. Aristotelian induction can make your choice more rational.

Exercise: Think back on a mistake you especially regret making. *What* exactly did you do? Next, what *caused* it—a lack of sleep, a temporary error in judgment, or a sudden "appetite" or mood swing? *Why* were you sleep deprived or moody? Finally, what's the *trend*? Was this error part of a pattern or a one-off? If the lapse is rare and not the sort of thing you usually do, then congratulations! You have proved your virtuous rule by that exception. If you see a trend, then this may be a sign of your final cause—your soul. Maybe you have a deeper need to explore.

Deduction: Turn Belief into Action

While induction gathers facts and draws a conclusion from them—making you think like a scientist, parsing reality through your powers of observation—deductive reasoning takes a shortcut. It skips the lab and fieldwork and goes right to the conclusion. Deduction does this by starting not with a fact but with a belief.

Aristotle invented rhetorical deduction by slimming down his infamous syllogism. You may be familiar with this three-beat chunk of logic that reads like a bad haiku:

All men are mortal.
Socrates is a man.
Therefore, Socrates is mortal.

The first line states a belief, something your audience agrees on or considers a certainty. "All men are mortal" is the *major premise*, stating a general belief. Human mortality is self-evident. Sure, the contrarian part of your audience may think, "What about Beyoncé? Isn't she immortal?" But then she's a goddess, not a man.

The second line, bringing Socrates into the picture, constitutes the *minor premise*, which gets to the specific case. Unlike Beyoncé, Socrates is a man. Those two lines push the audience inexorably toward the conclusion that Socrates is—wait for it—mortal!

When I first read Aristotle's *Prior Analytics*—hardly a page-turner but the starting gate for logic—it occurred to me that Socrates had died decades before Aristotle wrote that syllogism. So, while the logic seems flawless, the middle-line minor premise was technically untrue. Socrates had indeed proven himself mortal by dying. But was he still a man? Decades after he died, did he continue to wander Zombie-like through Athens? All humans in the present are alive. Socrates's life lies in the past. Therefore, Socrates is not human. Aristotle's syllogism carries a belief; but even Aristotle would have to admit that it represents a falsehood.

Why does this matter? And why should we care about syllogisms at all? Admittedly, they rank among Aristotle's most boring thoughts. Syllogisms state the obvious, then lead to the more obvious. But while we think that logic is indisputable, the truth is a good deal more slippery than we would like it to be.

All men are mortal? That depends on what you mean by "men." Pee-wee Herman was a man, sort of, but to me he'll live forever. Or do you mean literally mortal? In which case, are we simply referring to flesh and blood or should we consider what Socrates thought to be the immortal soul? Where does the truth lie? No matter how brutally, boringly logical we try to be, rhetoric—soul-bending persuasion—creeps through the cracks. While this seems a tragedy to the Spocks among us, for those of us trying to motivate ourselves, rhetoric is a gift from the gods.

Aristotle himself seemed to recognize that his deductive logic was not exactly airtight. Or at least he found that pure syllogistic logic failed to apply enough to day-to-day matters. Too many answers to life's questions begin with "That depends . . ." All men are mortal? That depends on whether you exclude the special Greeks whom the gods promoted to immortal status, such as the strong man Heracles—or (I love this story) a fisherman named Glaucus who ate an herb that transformed him into a sea god, fins and all.

Logic gets even scalier when it comes to making a decision or giving advice. A dad says, "Treasury bonds are the safest investment." The syllogism looks like this:

> The United States has always paid its debt.
> Treasury bonds are official U.S. debt.
> Therefore, Treasury bonds are safe.

Mom replies, "That depends on whether Congress eventually defaults on the debt." Conditions can change. What was true in the past may not be so true in the future. Aristotle himself recognized that life is full of contingencies, a cluster of *that depends* junctures. What's more, the first line of a syllogism rarely begins with an unchallengeable fact. The sky isn't always blue. Laughter can be a horrible medicine. You may not deserve a break today.

To deal with challengeable propositions, mutable circumstances, and our sorry, emotion-stained human nature, Aristotle came up with a syllogism 2.0, the **enthymeme**. Instead of three lines, he shortened the tool to just two, getting rid of that largely unnecessary middle one. ("Socrates is a man," duh.)

Here's a fine example of an enthymeme: "Looks like rain. We should bring an umbrella." If we rendered that statement as a classic syllogism, it would read:

The sky is showing signs of impending rain.
Rain will make us wet.
Therefore, we should carry a rain-shedding instrument.

When aliens finally visit us from outer space, you can imagine they will talk like that, assuming they don't like to get wet. But if they want to communicate with us mortal humans, they will need to learn the enthymeme. Aristotle wrote that the device begins with an "agreed premise or received opinion." In other words, it starts with something that your audience believes to be true at the moment. Or, when the subject deals with the future, the enthymeme begins with a probability—something likely to happen. "Looks like rain" is a probability. Your audience can deduce from this premise that an umbrella will be a wise choice.

Couldn't you use inductive logic to make the same argument?

Cumulonimbus clouds are rolling in, the wind is backing from the east, I smell moisture in the air, and my Weather Channel app says there's a 90 percent chance of rain. Therefore, we should bring an umbrella.

Sure, that makes a valid argument. But it uses a scientific approach, which relies on accumulated evidence to reach a tentative conclusion. If our purpose is to persuade an audience to bring an umbrella, the deductive enthymeme works best. Aristotle wrote that facts can persuade, but arguments by enthymeme "make more of an impression."

The enthymeme can similarly help us make a distinct impression on ourselves. It starts with a proof (*Looks like rain*) and goes right to the conclusion (*Bring an umbrella*). While this seems like another boring logical tool, the enthymeme carries with it a strange recursive power. Psychologically, the two lines are mutually persuasive. Even if you have a slight doubt that it will rain, the second line bends your mind toward the act of shedding rain with an umbrella. Your skepticism gets swept aside in your unconscious anticipation of bad weather.

Let's construct another enthymeme around Jeffrey "the Dude" Lebowski.

The Dude always abides. Therefore, I should mix a White Russian.

Deep down, Lebowski may harbor some doubts about his abidingness. In the rare sober moments when he contemplates his life of unemployment and bowling, he may even feel a twinge of existential despair. But his choice to make a cocktail reinforces his belief in being the abiding Dude. (You may have hated *The Big Lebowski*, but that's just, like, your opinion, man.) "The Dude abides" starts with Lebowski's belief in himself. Abiding is what he does, his final cause. He considers himself an artist of existence.

People also unconsciously state an enthymeme when they excuse themselves from a mission. "I don't dance" describes the belief in a soul that lacks rhythm or coordination. If this musically challenged soul were nerdy enough to state the second half of the enthymeme, he would add, "Therefore, I will not sign us up for ballroom dance lessons." While this enthymeme holds up logically, its premise—"I don't dance"—states a belief, not necessarily a verifiable fact.

Because enthymematic logic makes such an impression, this kind of deduction can enforce false beliefs about ourselves. "I can't stand sweating" turns the discomfort of working out into an existential impossibility. This is why it helps to know when you happen to be thinking deductively. What premise underlies your conclusion? Exactly how true is that premise? And does it necessarily lead to the conclusion? Sure, maybe our nondancer has never achieved more than a series of spasms at a dance party. But this does not make him incapable of learning an acceptable foxtrot.

The proof in an enthymeme is a stated or implied *because, since,* or *if*. The conclusion tends to reinforce our belief in the proof. Because the Dude abides, it is natural to his abidingness that he should mix a White Russian. The cocktail in return convinces the Dude himself that he happens to be one awesome abider.

The enthymeme's reinforcing effect can help us bend our souls toward more salutary beliefs:

I'm basically a kind person, so I should forgive that jerk.

The proof is your belief in your own basic kindness. That belief may not be airtight. If you think too hard about it, you may remember the times when you ignored homeless people, insulted your significant other, and retweeted a cruel meme. But when you deliberate over forgiving the jerk—the inevitable conclusion for your kind self—it makes you think, "Why, yes, I truly am kind!" Enthymemes tend to persuade in both directions. The proof leads to the conclusion, which makes the proof seem even more believable.

If we all consciously used the enthymeme, we might have more students applying to medical school. A great many aspirants screen themselves out when they balk at taking organic chemistry, the scariest of all undergraduate science courses. They want to be healers, not scientists calculating the valences of carbon molecules. An enthymeme based on their own self-belief could bend their souls away from their unscientific nature.

I'm good at jumping hurdles, so I'm going to jump this one.

The belief in overcoming obstacles—how else did the student get into this great college?—leads to the decision to take organic chem. In return, the thought of attempting this next obstacle, a feat of hurdle jumping that plays to her ability to jump hurdles, strengthens her belief in that ability.

The enthymeme could also get more shy people to go on dating apps. Start with a self-belief—say, that you're a fairly courageous person.

Because I have a lot of courage, I'm going to take the leap and meet up with a stranger.

Without that enthymeme, the thought of showing up in a public place and making awkward conversation with an attractive stranger seems terrifying. But set in the context of your ability to face fears, the idea of actually meeting a stranger makes you seem all the more courageous. The enthymeme forms a virtuous cycle.

You can use the enthymeme for any ambition—volunteering at a soup kitchen, changing careers, trekking in Nepal, whatever. Start with a core part of your character, something that reflects your truest, most soulful self.

I love turning my mind off. So why not do mindless chores in a soup kitchen?

> Exercise: Are you especially well organized? Then who better to plan a way to change careers? You can see what we're doing here. Think of something you would love to experience or accomplish—a goal you lack the

confidence to carry out. Then go through a catalog of your strengths. Find a strength that comes closest to making your decision seem possible. Then construct an enthymeme. If you don't absolutely believe in that relevant strength, or if you feel that your strength isn't that strong, try the enthymeme anyway. It just may make your strength seem stronger.

THE TOOLS

Induction. This half of logic examines just the facts, ma'am, before reaching a conclusion. Aristotle broke this process down into four "causes": *material, efficient, formal,* and *final*. Here's an easier way to interpret a fact, experience, or piece of news: (1) What is it? (2) What caused it? (3) Why is it? (4) What's the trend? Just by engaging the rational part of our brain, we can keep ourselves from panicking about the state of the world— or the state of our finances, for that matter.

Deduction. While inductive logic starts with the evidence, deduction begins with a "truth." In rhetoric, truth is a matter of belief. The guy proudly singing off-key in a karaoke bar is no gifted tenor. But to him, his belief in his singing ability is the same as the God-given truth—at least so long as the beer holds up. His belief has given him the courage to get up there and bellow "Don't Stop Believin'." Our singer is perfectly logical in spite of his lager-enabled delusion. He believes himself to be an awesome singer; so why shouldn't he share his gift with the others in the bar?

Enthymeme. The karaoke singer's logic takes the form of Aristotle's two-part deductive tool—consisting of proof in the form of a belief, and a conclusion. *I'm a great singer. Therefore, I should get up and sing.* The enthymeme's self-persuasive power lies in its recursive effect: The conclusion helps reinforce the belief. Our singer, motivated by his trust in his musical talent, staggers to the microphone. This act in turn reinforces his belief. Why else would he get up in front of these strangers?

But the enthymeme's recursion can work to block as well as motivate. A student tells herself, "I can't do math," and skips the calculus elective. See? That proves she can't do math. The secret to making the enthymeme work for us is to start with a positive belief. Sure, our student has struggled with math in the past. But she also once struggled to shoot baskets and has now made the team. "I'm brilliant with struggles," she tells herself. Which gives her the motivation to sign up for calculus. (In later chapters, we'll deal with failure.)

8

Framing

Define Your Life

Rhetoric's loose-handled spade

"The true and the approximately true are apprehended by the same faculty."

—Aristotle, *Rhetoric*

At this point, no one would blame you for feeling leery about rhetoric. Even Aristotle's rational *logos* can seem manipulative, because, well, it is. All this talk of soul-bending rhetoric contradicts Plato, who collared reality and made it stay in place. Plato argued that everything boils down to *forms* and can be described with just one definition. A spade is a spade. It has the form of a spade. Any other interpretation is just the shadow we see from Plato's nasty cave.

Aristotle obviously saw things differently. What is the "form" of the spade, besides the fact that it's hard to remember whether a spade is a trowel or a shovel? A spade is a gardening implement, clearly. But in a police procedural it can be a deadly weapon, a piece of evidence, or a clue. A spade can be a symbol on a playing card. The holy *Oxford English Dictionary* tells us that a spade can be "the gummy or wax-like matter secreted at the corner of the eye," a eunuch, the act of removing a female animal's ovaries, or "a male deer in its third year." And still we expect people to call a spade . . . well, you know. The Greek historian Plutarch writes of the enemy Macedonians:

> Phillipus answered that the Macedonians were fellows of no fine wit in their terms, but altogether gross, clubbish, and rustical, as they who had not the wit to call a spade by any other name than a spade.

Go ahead and call a spade a spade. Or, if you prefer, call anyone who calls a spade a spade "gross, clubbish, and rustical." Aristotle understood that life is complicated. Not everyone sits in the same cave. We see the shadows and forms of reality from different perspectives.

Years ago, a Dartmouth student named Emily Hill got caught in a blizzard while on a bus tour in the mountains of China. Being an experienced outdoorswoman and the only passenger who could speak Cantonese, Emily helped lead the others to safety without serious injury, except for some pretty severe cases of frostbite. Two weeks later, Emily was gored by a rhinoceros while hiking through Nepal's Chitwan National Park. She was a hardy young woman, and as you might have guessed, she recovered quickly. Within a week, Jane Pauley of the *Today* show was interviewing Emily in Nepal and her relieved parents in Kansas City over a satellite link.

Emily later told me that the most interesting thing about her crises was the totally different reactions among friends of her parents in Kansas City and her fellow Dartmouth students. Her parents' friends said, "See what happens when you let your daughter wander abroad?" Meanwhile, back on campus, students moaned, "Man, I wish I'd had such an experience!" Emily's elders saw one spade. The spade her classmates pictured was a very different implement.

One of the biggest problems we have in dealing with our own reality is our natural tendency to use terms thoughtlessly. We vote for a candidate who promises to create jobs. Great, but what's a job? Merely a source of income? Why can't that candidate push for laws that provide incomes without work? According to Elon Musk, that would be doable given enough robots. But robots take away our jobs. Or is a job simply work you have to do most days? In which case, is parenting a job? Did enslaved people have jobs? Do robots?

This kind of rabbit-hole cogitation can be extremely annoying, even disturbing. You might say it literally cost Socrates, the original definition sleuth, his life. But Aristotle believed that defining our terms can make life more meaningful. While inductive logic gathers facts on a rational trail toward a conclusion and deduction takes a belief and applies it to a situation, the logic of definition goes straight to the meaning.

In rhetoric, that meaning can incline in a direction that benefits the speaker most. You don't work at a job; you work for a cause! Sure, that work may entail an endless round of mind-numbing meetings, but you're advancing civilization by helping the economy, or enhancing knowledge, or keeping order through . . . don't call it paperwork; call it communicative organization.

Defining an issue forms a key aspect of **framing**, a system that allows you to gain the high ground on any subject. Framing starts with the definition of the issue. When you find yourself embroiled in an argument, a great way to throw your opponent off-balance is to ask, "What's this really about?" and then suggest a different definition. If your significant other goes ballistic about the way you load the dishwasher and you respond with "What's this really about?" you're asking for the frame. Is this spat about your dishwasher-loading failure, or about something that happened to him at work?

Why Meanings Are So Meaningful

Framing works in part by redefining an issue, creating a different meaning out of a situation or debate. For that reason, this book contains a strong dose of etymology—the study of word meanings and origins. While my passion for the *Oxford English Dictionary* may seem eccentric or even annoying (or so my wife will remind me after a dinner party), there is method to this etymological madness. All of philosophy and rhetoric began with the meaning of words. In the Bible, labeling reality became the first human act. After God created Adam, he formed birds and beasts from the ground; then the deity brought them straight to the man to see what he would name them. The book of Genesis goes on to say that Adam and Eve's descendants spoke "one language with the same words." They settled in a land called Shinar and began to build a great city with a brick tower so high it reached the heavens. God came to take a gander.

> And the Lord said, "Look, they are one people, and they have all one language, and this is only the beginning of what they will do; nothing that they propose to do will now be impossible for them."

God took extreme measures, demoting his clever species by breaking up the one language into many, confusing the people so that they couldn't cooperate on that threatening creation. According to the Bible, the place became known as Babel, from the Hebrew word *balal,* meaning "confusion."

Even when we technically speak the same language, we humans tend to create our own confused city of Babel by attaching different meanings to the same words. Even the word *meaning* can cause Babel-level confusion. What should we do to make our lives more "meaningful"? Check every item off our bucket list? Gain the highest rank at work? Win a Nobel Prize? Find love? These might be worthy goals, but what do they have to do with *meaning*? Before we can begin to make our plans, we really should settle on the meaning of meaning.

The early philosophers focused on meaning as a way of understanding reality and their place within it. Socrates wandered around Athens asking for meanings; the Socratic method is all about finding definitions. Plato's cave, whose inhabitants saw only the shadows of reality, had a Babel-esque aspect to it; our usual language often fails to see the world as it is. Plato wanted to drill through language right down to the form (*eidos* in Greek), the ultimate essence of everything. What, he asked, is the dogness of dogs, the mountainness of mountains, or the truest meanings of *courage, love,* and *goodness*? For that matter, what is the humanness of humans?

That last question inspired Aristotle's theory of the soul, an individual's ultimate character. Eventually, this pursuit of the truth of words led to modern branches of philosophy such as semantics, semiotics, and metaphysics. You could argue that all of philosophy is a search for meaning. Why else would anyone become a philosopher?

Mapping Your Personal Reality

People who love the outdoors often reframe cold, wind, and rain by annoying their companions with, "There's no bad weather. Only bad clothing." Oscar Wilde, for his part, defined nature as "a damp place where birds fly about uncooked." He built a rhetorical frame, a kind of window that showed the reality he wanted us to see.

Actually, I wish there were a better term. Framing does not put a frame around things; instead, it shifts an issue from one topic to another. At least that's how the ancient Greeks thought about the device. Permit me a bit more word-nerding. Remember that *topic* has the same Greek root as *topological:* the ancient Greek word *topos,* meaning "place." When you make a point, you stake a claim on a topic. Framing puts a fence around the claim you have staked.

Political consultants like to say that when you own the frame, you own the issue. *This bill isn't about feeding children; it's about liberals wanting more big government!* Or: *Banning abortions is about controlling women's bodies!* The same goes for owning our personal issues. Benjamin Franklin found superior wisdom in his gout. He wrote a dialogue in the voice of the ailment, which admonished the man himself for complaining of the pain: "Is it not I who, in the character of your physician, have saved you from the palsy, dropsy, and apoplexy? One or the other of which would have done for you long ago but for me." With that dialogue, Franklin shifted pain into a helpful aid to self-discipline.

Framing can even bend our souls toward a somewhat different definition of ourselves. When P. T. Barnum was a four-year-old in rural Connecticut, his grandfather gave him his own farm, Ivy Island. At the age of ten, his parents finally allowed him to see it. It turned out to be swampland. "The truth flashed upon me," he later wrote in his autobiography. "I had been the laughing-stock of the family and neighborhood for years." He went on to become one of the greatest hucksters in history. Thus, he reframed what could have been a traumatic experience—how could he ever trust his loved ones?—into a lesson on hucksterism.

But framing entails more than simply changing the meaning of words and our interpretation of an issue. The strategy follows a few steps.

First, you want to **broaden the issue.** In politics, framing consultants expanded the minimum wage into enabling Americans to live on what they earn. Abortion bans grew into a "culture of life," and guns became home security. We already did some issue broadening in the previous chapters, when we expanded an organic chem course into a life-challenging hurdle and dating into a self-affirming test of strength.

The next step in framing is to *simplify* a topic within that broadened setting, then *make the issue personal*. Rachel Carson did this brilliantly. For a book describing how the chemical DDT thinned the eggshells of raptors, she chose the title *Silent Spring*. This frame broadened the issue from the side effects of an agricultural chemical to the entire world, while simplifying and personalizing it to your own backyard, bereft of bird calls. The mental effect on readers is almost cinematic. With that frame, our internal camera moves through a laboratory with white-coated chemists, cuts to a farm field where an airplane sprays a scary white mist, and zooms in on a tree at the end of the field where a hawk sits on her eggs. Cut to a backyard where a mother hangs her laundry (the book came out in 1962) and all we hear is . . . silence. She looks up, listens. Oh, that awful DDT!

Eight years later, Madison Avenue created a public-service ad for the Keep America Beautiful antilittering organization. It shows an actor, Iron Eyes Cody, playing a native American paddling a birchbark canoe through trash-filled water while factories spew smoke in the background. He pulls up onto a shore speckled with plastic and steps out of his canoe. A load of trash gets thrown from a passing car and lands right in front of the man's deerskin moccasins. The camera now moves in on his stoic, lined face, and we see a single tear emerge from his eye.

This is classic framing: the careless act of littering gets broadened into a sin and then personalized into the mythical portrayal of a people who respect the land. Even better from a persuasion perspective, the ad triggered an emotional reframe in the audience. Our mighty planet suddenly seemed vulnerable, just like that Native American. Indians don't cry! The ad—since condemned for its stereotypical portrayal—ran countless times during the seventies, and it arguably led to widespread support for the environmental movement. That decade saw federal passage of the Endangered Species Act, the Superfund program, the Clean Air and Clean Water acts, the EPA, the removal of lead from gasoline . . . and the banning of DDT.

If a reframed insecticide and tragic litter can do all that, imagine what reframing can do for your own self-inflicted pain and agony. All we have to do is make a frame that helps us suffer pain and agony. Fun!

Suffering: Welcome the Sting

We Americans have a weird, even kinky relationship with pain. We spend $24 billion a year avoiding it. We equate effort with pain—*no pain, no gain*—while buying any workout or diet that promises painless results. If we can find a creative way to reframe that pain and make ourselves believe in the new frame, we can help eliminate a very big, uncomfortable obstacle to our willingness to go through the necessary discomfort of change.

In search of pain reframing, I went back to my source of spiritual inspiration, the *Oxford English Dictionary*. What's the word for undergoing pain? *To suffer*. Like many of our language's more miserable words—*prison, torture, abattoir, bayonet, coup d'état, espionage, mutiny, rout*—*suffer* comes from the French. The Norman invaders brought with them more *agonie* than *joie de vivre*, apparently. They could not have been pleasant occupiers. (*Occupy* also comes from the French, *naturellement*.) These etymologies convey the sense that the British Isles were doing pretty well before the Normans brought all that misery, along with the word *miserable*, to make sure everyone knew how *horrible* (French word) everything was. Maybe Americans' passion for pain relief is a cultural post-traumatic reaction to having suffered the Normans.

Still, the French left us with something useful. To suffer means to submit, undergo, bear, or allow. The legendary marathoner Steve Prefontaine famously said that while he was not the best natural runner, no one could suffer more. He could beat more talented athletes by withstanding more pain for longer stretches.

But the word implies more than a long-term submission to pain; and here's where things get interesting and even useful. Generations of Christian children in Sunday school have been confused by the line in the King James Bible where Jesus "suffered" the children to come unto him. Was he annoyed by the loud, whiny youngsters? Possibly. But the seventeenth-century translators meant *suffer* to mean "allow," as in permit. *Go on, let 'em come.* This hardly counts as an enthusiastic endorsement of children, but Jesus did not seem to think they were the worst cross to bear.

This interpretation of suffering—allowing in pain, discomfort, or inconvenient children—could help you and me feel a little less sorry for ourselves. I left out pity in the pathos chapter, because I was saving it for the cure. We can alleviate self-pity by reframing it. Start with the definition. Pity, Aristotle said, is "a certain pain occasioned by an apparently destructive evil occurring to one who does not deserve it." Many readers over the centuries have been annoyed by his frequent use of the word "apparently." But everything in Aristotle is about the appearances, particularly when he's writing about rhetoric. The pain is caused not by evil but by our interpretation of it.

In this case, he was writing about the pity a person has for someone else. The emotion tends to be stronger if the pitier feels likely to suffer the same thing himself; there but by the grace of God. In Aristotle's definition, this makes self-pity the strongest emotion of all.

Many of the methods we use to motivate ourselves are supposed to deal with suffering: the literal pain of a workout, the virtual pain of a forgone martini, or an introvert's social pain from meeting strangers at a party. The answer to self-pity, the ancients believed, was to view suffering as a kind of skill. Since then, some of our most impressive feats have resulted from the same attitude.

Some years ago, *Outside* magazine ran a piece titled "The King of the Ferret Leggers." It profiled a seventy-two-year-old Yorkshireman named Reg Mellor, who was the undisputed champion of a deservedly obscure sport. Each contestant tied his pant legs at the ankles and then dropped a pair of ferrets down his trousers. The point was to see how long he could withstand these ill-tempered, sharp-toothed mammals. The record had been stuck at forty seconds before Mellor smashed it with an uncanny five hours and twenty-six minutes. The writer suggested that the feat must have taken a great deal of courage and concentration. "Naw, noon o' that," Mellor said. "You just got to be able ta have your tool bitten and not care." While some of us are inclined to pity the ferrets more than the Yorkshireman, you have to hand it to Reg Mellor. He was a certified world champion of suffering. We can use some of this skill to bear the pains of life without lapsing into demotivational self-pity. It simply requires a bit of reframing, which, as we've seen, goes like this: **redefine, broaden, focus.**

Let us take an extreme scenario. You decide to keep bees. Imagine making your own honey, creating a clever label (Gold Rush?), with the goal of gifting jars and beeswax candles to admiring friends and loved ones. One problem: You harbor a mortal terror of stings. Do you quit and take up knitting? No, you doughty Aristotelian, you do not! Instead, you broaden the issue by turning stings into the debt you owe your apian collaborators. After all, the attacking bees sacrifice their own lives to defend the hives, all while doing most of the production work. Bearing a sting or two is the least you can do. You learn from a beekeeper to expect a dozen stings in your first season, while you're getting the hang of smokers and protective clothing. Now we zoom in on a single sting. While the bee will die, poor thing, your own passing pain will compose one twelfth of the debt repaid. Besides, that pain will not just make the stings that follow more bearable; bee sting pain just may make you better at feeling pain in general. You will become a skilled sufferer.

Useful Fallacy: Post Hoc

When I implied that a crying Native American led directly to revolution in environmental law and activism, I was deploying one of my favorite logical peccadillos: *post hoc, ergo propter hoc.* After this, therefore because of this. A baseball player scores a home run while wearing his girlfriend's charm bracelet. From then on, he borrows her bracelet for every game. He scored after the first time he put on the bracelet; therefore, the bracelet charmed the game!

You need not be superstitious to use the post hoc fallacy on yourself. Simply begin attributing any little success, any gain toward your goal, to something you did earlier. A piano student struggles to play a chromatic scale until one day, as he sits down at the keyboard, his fingers brush across his pants. Shortly after, he finally plays a proper scale. From then on, he brushes his pants before playing.

Or suppose you happen to be bad at remembering names. You run across a new neighbor on the street, and just as you begin to panic—*what was her name?*—you find yourself looking straight at her nose, and out of the blue you remember: "Hey, Zarya!" From then on, you glance subtly at people's noses before coming up with their names. It's your own fallacious rabbit's-foot memory charm.

Yes, of course it's stupid. Fallacies are stupid. But their very stupidity helps us set our brains to the Homer Simpson state of cognitive ease. You need not even believe it entirely. The schnozz-enabled memory trick may simply make you smile, and that cognitive easing alone can help you persuade yourself that you're not so bad at names after all.

Trace any good thing back to what you did before it, then remember to do that same thing as your own post hoc charm. Fallaciousness at its best.

Useful Fallacy: Antecedent

This one is a close relation to post hoc, because it happily reframes a pattern. The *fallacy of antecedent* has to do with the belief that, because something has not yet happened, it never will. Or something that has always happened always will. Have you noticed how people who drive a route to work tend to go much faster than those who drive the same route less often? Rush hour turns otherwise sane people into NASCAR drivers. The more they drive this commute, the less risky it seems, and the faster they go. They have avoided any accidents, and so they think—consciously or otherwise—they always will.

On a grander scale, the ancient Romans operated a successful republic for hundreds of years, meeting every external crisis as well as internal ones, and so they believed that their system would go on forever. You can understand why, when Julius Caesar destroyed the republic, it came as a big shock. Commuters and Romans stand guilty of the same logical crime: thinking that the life they're used to will go on forever.

The fallacy might keep you from making any sort of change. You didn't in the past, so you won't in the future. But, as with any sort of rhetoric, you need to control the frame. Your past experiments haven't led to disaster, so this one won't either. Or else pick something that has always happened and make it analogous to something you want to happen. The fallacy lets us select patterns in our own life and apply them to our goal. Think of your good habits or commitments, the things you seem to have been doing forever. Now apply them to your goal.

You've been in a successful relationship for ten years, despite being buffeted with moves and other crises; this proves you can hold a steady course in the midst of change. You've always stuck with your lover, through rich and poor, better and worse, and always will. Clearly, you'll never let the setbacks from a positive life change hold you back. Or, to take something only apparently trivial, suppose you are the one in the family who loads the dishwasher. You have always done it, so you always will. There is a reason why you are the dishwasher-loader in the family. You are an organizer.

You see patterns, can make things fit together in ways that would challenge the non-dishwasher-loader. This should give you the confidence to see your path through the chaos of a life change.

Useful Fallacy: False Analogy

Let's say you do this one thing—dishwasher loading—perfectly. Therefore, you might believe that you can do something analogous just as well. For example, perhaps your dishwasher prowess proves your incomparable talent for organization and problem solving. Remember that when you're thinking about applying for a job that requires creative solutions for managing projects.

In rhetoric, actually, unlikely analogies aren't a fallacy at all. When you apply a skill like dishwasher organization to your work life, you engage in **analogical thinking**—the ability to connect unlike things to boost your confidence and creativity. Ancient Greek philosophers, along with the early Buddhists, were big on connections. Everything in the universe is linked. Video-game addicts have made brilliant drone pilots. Class clowns have turned their mouth noises into beatbox careers.

Useful Fallacy: Hasty Generalization

This one is the opposite of the fallacy of antecedent: You commit a hasty generalization whenever you interpret a single instance as a trend. A mouse scurries across your kitchen floor, and you panic at the thought of a mouse infestation: thousands of rodents eating you out of house and home! Like every other fallacy, this one can be turned into a helpful tool of illogic. A coordination-challenged kid in gym class tries again and again to shoot a basketball from the foul line, ignoring the jeers of his classmates. On the verge of quitting, fighting back tears, he makes one final half-blind heave and . . . swish. Well, hey! Maybe he's good at basketball after all. His odds of succeeding a second time have just increased greatly.

Hasty generalization flips exceptions that prove the rule. The fallacy takes an exception and *makes* it the rule. One push-up proves you are brilliant at push-ups. You turn down dessert once, and that confirms your awesome discipline.

Useful Fallacy: Appeal to Popularity

All the other kids do it, so why can't you? Role models and influencers depend on this excellent fallacy. To use the popularity appeal to our benefit, we hang out with people we admire and mimic their actions. If you want to get better at tennis, invite better players. To get wittier, find wittier friends. The appearance of those around you becomes the norm. Placing yourself, and your soul, in a different rhetorical setting composes the ultimate reframe.

Useful Fallacy: The Unit Fallacy

I love this one, because it warps reality in infinite ways. I recently made a trip to London, where I bought small gifts to stuff into family stockings at Christmas. Everything was so cheap! Afterward, I treated myself to a meal at a fast-casual restaurant that cost just twelve pounds. Pounds, dollars, they're pretty much the same thing, right? Not until I got home did I look up the exchange rate. A pound was worth 30 percent more than a dollar. I had committed the unit fallacy, which confuses apples with oranges, pounds with dollars. So why am I happy with this fallacy? Because it enabled me to get beyond my usual cheapskate, miserly self. My generosity was spurred by beautifully bad math.

That same fallacy led me to attempt the single greatest athletic feat of my life, when I decided to become the first person over fifty ever to run up a certain mountain in fewer minutes than I was old in years.

Reframing and happy fallacies will not work if you think too rationally about them. Notice that all the tools so far have a common theme: They twist time and patterns, evidence and significance, proofs and conclusions—all in the noble service of bending your soul.

THE TOOLS

<u>Framing.</u> Change the definition, broaden the issue, then simplify or personalize.

The tombstone for the late Jared Bates, erected in 1800, reads: "His Widow Aged 24 who mourns as one who can be comforted lives at 7 Elm Street this village and possesses every qualification for a Good Wife." The carving neatly reframes a memorial as an advertisement. These days, the widow Bates would undoubtedly have made an awesome influencer.

<u>Fallacies.</u> Logic, like good grammar or an erect posture, begs for a vacation. As Aristotle himself pointed out, none of us contains the perfectly rational soul that he would want us to have. By straying from the logical straight and narrow, we can take our self-beliefs in a different direction, creating faith in ourselves that we otherwise couldn't achieve. So let yourself believe that when something happened, it caused something else (post hoc). You do something well, therefore you should do something

slightly similar equally well (false analogy). Something happened, so it proved it will always happen (hasty generalization). Something has always happened, so it always will (antecedent). Everyone around you does it, so you should too (appeal to popularity). All this was measured by a number, and that number applies to any unit (unit fallacy).

Part 3

ACTION

9

Habit

Adjust Your Routine

Aristotle's Tortoise Method

"The question is asked whether happiness is to be acquired by learning or by habituation or some other sort of training..."

—Aristotle, *Nicomachean Ethics*

If you want to know how Aristotle would describe your character, eat dessert—preferably the kind of chocolate geological event described on the restaurant menu as a sin. If you were trying to maintain a low-sugar diet, Aristotle would not judge you by the decadence of the dessert but by the amount of guilt you felt afterward. If you believed you deserved the treat, or simply ate it because you wanted to, he would call you self-indulgent. If you felt guilty—you just couldn't help scarfing down that whole gooey mess—then Aristotle would say you were "incontinent."

Chances are, you are not a self-indulgent person; if you were, you might be happily binge-watching *Too Hot to Handle* with a side of Oreos instead of reading this. But most of us are "incontinent" to some degree. We know the right things to do, but we succumb to the temptations that surround us.

The essential problem, Aristotle said, is a disconnection between our ends and our means. Our animal instincts often wander from our goals, away from what he called the "ruling part" of ourselves. We wish to be fit, healthy, and productive, yet we make choices that fail to reach those ends. We become happy only when we align our wishes with the means to achieve happiness. So, okay, how on earth do we consistently make the right choices? Aristotle's advice: don't. You need not act like a saint every moment. The trick is to limit the number of choices we must make. This does not mean avoiding decisions. It means sticking to the prudent ones.

We're talking about habits. The subject may seem mundane coming from Aristotle, the man who invented logic and tutored Alexander the Great. But habits are more than a means to fitness and productivity. Aristotle believed that choicelessness is a crucial key to happiness.

This might sound positively un-American. After all, we enjoy the most self-indulgent culture on the planet, where the snack food aisle might as well have been guaranteed somewhere in the Constitution. But you also know that making choices—especially those that fall on the continuum from good-for-you to avoid-the-doctor—is stressful. To be happy, Aristotle implied, we need to put much of our life on autopilot. This principle made him the first great evangelist of daily habits.

I've come across other habit evangelists over the years, but one particularly stands out in my memory. Back when I was young and single, I visited a dentist's office that employed an attractive young hygienist. Halfway through scraping my tartar, she nudged my arm with her hip. "Know what I like to do with my dates?"

I shook my head.

"I floss them." She nodded toward the little sink, and I spat into it.

"You floss them?"

"I do, I floss them. If they don't let me, there's no second date."

"Huh." In my dating life I had met some . . . interesting women but had not yet experienced one with a flossing jones.

She resumed cleaning my teeth. "You can tell a lot about a person by their gums. What kind of lives they lead. People lie, but their gums don't." She reached over for the dental floss and broke off a section, lovingly wrapping it around her long fingers. "Your gums," she said, squinting into my mouth, "aren't bad at all. I bet you don't even bleed."

Were we flirting? Did she consider this appointment a sort of dental advanced placement, allowing us to skip the relationship's flossing stage? I'll never know; she gave me her number, but I didn't call it. Still, you might say that her gum-centric test of a date's virtue counted as Aristotelian. My decent gums revealed a soul capable of at least one steady habit. It so happened that I had been flossing for so many years that it seemed a necessary bedtime ritual. This, in both Aristotle's and the hygienist's terms, was a sign of virtue.

The Unexciting Upside of Being Regular

Humans are already a habitual species; only cats seem more regular than we are. Unlike cats, we are also extraordinarily adaptable;

we can get used to almost anything. What seems ghastly at first eventually becomes natural, even de rigueur. If you had somehow never heard of flossing, and someone introduced you to the idea of taking a string and painstakingly forcing it into every tiny gap between your teeth, the chore would seem arduous and a little disgusting. But do it every evening, year after year, and it becomes robotic, even necessary to your identity—a perfect alignment between your daily self and your gum-preserving soul.

Admittedly, this adaptability can turn life bland. When you travel to a new city, try this experiment: Ride public transportation to the suburbs and back just to see what it might feel like for a resident. Some commutes—the Seattle ferry to Bainbridge Island, with its spectacular view of Mount Rainier, or the Metro-North railroad line that follows the beautiful Connecticut coast to New York City—seem like miniature cruises. Yet the notable thing about being a guest commuter in these places is how little people pay attention to the ride. This is understandable; most of the passengers have gotten used to it. But it still seems amazing when you ride the Yellow Line Metro over the Potomac River in Washington, D.C., and see no one look up from their smartphone to gaze at the spectacular views of the monuments. The regular commute takes something special and turns it into the everyday.

Our daily meals can take on this same aspect of commuting. Give a donut to a two-year-old and you'll see pure passion. Stop by a Dunkin' for a Boston cream every morning, on the other hand, and it offers little more indulgent pleasure than a good floss.

But adaptability has its upside. Yes, it might extract color from our lives, but it also holds the secret to turning bad habits into good ones. Replace the donut with a protein bar for the first time, and it feels like a letdown you really don't need that early in the morning. But continue for a month to swap protein for cream fill-ing, and never mind what it does to your body; the bar seems just as naturally boring as the donut once did. Keep it up for a year, and the thought of an early morning donut might seem unnatural, even stomach-turning.

The hard part is to get to that quotidian stage. Aristotle considered the act of sacrificing instant pleasure for a long-term goal to be a form of courage. But do this with your good habits, and that courage becomes a kind of super-habit all its own. People who are into CrossFit, the competitive workout system, have a slogan: *Embrace the suck*. Welcome the pain that leads to gain, and it becomes a habitual part of your identity. Reaching that point, though, requires courage all its own.

Aristotle distinguished between the courage to embrace the suck and the habit of avoiding temptations. Resisting passing pleasures is its own virtue; he called it "temperance." The temperate person avoids seconds and skips dessert. She drives a sensible car and never goes outside without sunscreen. She does not embrace the suck so much as avoid life's harmful allurements. The courageous person seeks ways to replace bad habits with good ones. The temperate person never acquires bad habits in the first place.

At our best, we tend to embody a mix of the two. But temperance and courage make sense only if steady habits and suck embracing lead to happiness. Michael Pollan, author of *The Omnivore's Dilemma* and a champion of temperate nutrition, once made the mistake of appearing on the NPR show *Wait Wait . . . Don't Tell Me!* The comedian Paula Poundstone offered a contrarian view of nutrition. "One of the things that has made my life worth living is Ring Dings," she told him.

Pollan conceded that an occasional Ring Ding wouldn't kill her. The ultraprocessed pastries counted as "special occasion foods," he said.

"What the hell's the matter with you?" Poundstone retorted. "I said it's what makes my life worth living. You may know a lot about food, but you don't know the first thing about living, buddy."

Aristotle might accuse Poundstone of being self-indulgent. But if Ring Dings really are her soul's delight, who are we to tell her to switch to fiber? Poundstone is no fool. She undoubtedly knows what Ring Dings do to her gut biota. But she embraces that suck in her pursuit of the meaningful life, which clearly includes snack cakes. Okay, maybe she's just rationalizing the fact that she gives in to temptation. But you could also say the woman shows courage.

The Lure: Sex and Honey

Aristotle wrote that in order to get an audience to commit to a goal, we need to make the end seem wonderfully desirable, and the means to reach it appear easily doable. First, dangle the lure, which is the shining goal. Then show how easy the steps seem to be. We can call this method the **Lure & Ramp.**

The lure usually requires some reframing. Advertisers reframe products into lures as a sex-enabled bait and switch. Sex—do I need to tell you this?—may constitute the greatest rhetorical lure of all. To sell an impractical car to a heterosexual man, they pose a woman next to the car. *Buy the car, testosterone-challenged man, and . . .* the thinking pretty much stops at the groin level.

By now we have gotten used to the fact that *logos* does not have to limit itself to straight-line reasoning. We can see the same Madison Avenue technique in celebrity product endorsements, a method Aristotle called "witnessing."

The goal: Hawk a ridiculously expensive mechanical timepiece that is slightly less accurate than a ten-dollar quartz watch.

The lure: John Travolta. You too can be as cool and sexy as this watch-wearing jet pilot / dancer / actor!

Enough about models and actors. Let's imagine you want to improve your health. You do, don't you? Sex works there, too.

The goal: getting healthier.

The lure: getting a relationship.

Picture this: A man declares himself not to be a morning person, considering it a badge of honor never to have seen a sunrise. But then he gets invited for a dawn jog with the most beautiful single woman in the neighborhood. Setting an early alarm now sounds rather tolerable. Given a sufficient emotional incentive, even the most stubborn mind can change. This night owl loves the idea of spending quality time with the attractive woman. Still, would this lure be shiny enough for him to lay out running clothes, set the alarm to go off in the dark, adjust his appearance to make himself less of a gargoyle, find his way down a scary darkened block to the meeting point, and then actually run?

This is where the second part of Aristotle's method kicks in: the ramp.

The Ramp: Don the Shorts

Without our human instinct for easy ways out, the diet industry would go bust. Motivation usually requires the appearance of a high gain-to-pain ratio—an irresistible lure and a seemingly easy approach to it. To accomplish anything painful, we need to make the effort seem less steep, turning a long process into a series of simple steps.

Following this make-it-easy philosophy, our lovestruck night owl divvies up his running mission, splitting a daunting task into tiny chores. Before going to bed, he says to himself, "I'll just set out my best workout shorts and T-shirt."

Then: "I'm just setting my alarm. No big deal."

Then, when the alarm goes off next morning: "Stand up. Just stand."

Then bathroom, toothbrush.

Then squirm into the clothes already laid out, no thought required.

Then: "Well, since I'm dressed . . ." and he heads out the door.

Getting up at a ridiculous hour to pound half-naked through a darkened neighborhood can sound daunting. But each step is a no-brainer. Persuading your audience, including your soul, requires making every individual action seem easy.

Suppose you can barely play a passable "Moonlight Sonata" on the piano, but for some reason you keep dreaming about playing standards in some classy downtown restaurant. You may very well not want to, but let's stay with it for a bit. Even someone who burns with ambition to play "Sweet Caroline" for drunken patrons likely finds the effort formidable. Two years of pain and agony, of scales and music theory and contrapuntal rhythms, all while your loved ones frown and put on headphones? How can you possibly motivate yourself to put in all that effort?

Aristotle would say you don't have to. You just need to be willing to do a little bit, then a little more. Instead of scaling a vast wall of effort, you take a tiny step up the incline of work. Picturing yourself hearing applause as five-dollar bills fill your request jar: This is the lure. To pursue it, you provide yourself a ramp. As the perfectly true cliché goes, big achievements come in small steps.

The Lure & Ramp lies at the heart of a very old sales technique, and we see it in daily use today. To get you to buy a virtual reality headset, for example, a salesperson will not talk about the price or even the technical wizardry. She'll simply invite you to try it on. She discovers that you care little for video games and prefer nature hikes to thrill rides, so she offers you the virtual experience of paddling a canoe down the Amazon. Instead of urging you to buy the device, she might simply ask for your email so she can update you on the latest nature adventures being developed for the headset. While she could try to sell you her cheapest set now, patience offers her a greater chance at a bigger sale eventually. The headset trial and five-minute Amazon adventure let her dangle the lure of amazing global experiences. Your email address is the first small step toward an expensive purchase.

While the Lure & Ramp obviously works in sales, how can you use the technique on yourself? Through chunking. Your goal—or rather, your vision of succeeding at it—provides the lure. To create a ramp, you break the achievement down into the smallest possible efforts.

We should think of any skill or accomplishment as a plan, with each step an easy and even attractive bit of doable exertion. And if some of those steps, or those many hours, seem painful, then consider that the effort builds your strength in suffering.

> Exercise: Think of a project or goal that has had you procrastinating forever. Chunk it into ridiculously short

lengths. For instance, if you need to write a report or large memo without using AI, make the first chunk cleaning the screen of your computer. Next, choose the font. Then write the topic sentence and rewrite it six times. Next, get some coffee. Each one of these chunks can count as an accomplishment.

Your Very Own Time Zone

While Paula Poundstone may be happy with her sugar-fueled habits, the rest of us mortals have patterns we would rather change. This often takes more courage than we have at any moment. Having decided on a particular goal—better health, a soul-pleasing body, more books read, a new craft—we turn into Macbeth, unable to screw our courage to the sticking-place. (Lady Macbeth was using military jargon to goad her husband into action; a crossbow was ready to fire when the archer turned the screw far enough. I couldn't resist the etymology. Call me incontinent.)

Aristotle had an answer to this courage problem. Instead of tackling the big pains, he proposed chunking them into smaller, more tolerable bits of suffering. We've encountered this already. Focus on the glorious goal—the lure—then convince yourself that achieving it will not be that terribly hard. Aristotle's ramp consists of the small things you do for that goal, carried out with disciplined regularity—habits, in other words. To make them tolerable, the ramp must involve *small* habits. You can gain them bit by bit, with one habit building off the previous one. Consider this method a kind of ratchet, in which you secure one habit before adding the next, until eventually your habits have gone all the way to the sticking place and you take full aim at your goal.

You might prefer a less violent metaphor. Call it the **Tortoise Method.** Just as the Tortoise in Aesop's fable persistently plods to the finish line, leaving behind the cocky, self-indulgent hare, habit building works best in the slow lane. The Tortoise Method starts with the easiest steps, then builds with more easy steps. In my case, my desire was to get fit and maybe even see myself as a sort of athlete. I wanted to go on trail runs with younger people without embarrassing myself. To accomplish this goal, I would need to lose considerable weight, get aerobically fit, and gain strength beyond my Gumby-with-a-gut body. All that would require a cluster of habits, none of which seemed the least bit attractive.

The first obstacle faced by my tortoise self was time. You doubtless have the same problem: Our days are already overscheduled with work and other obligations. How can we take on still more? I thought, *If only I could conjure an hour, magically creating a twenty-five-hour day, then I would have a window for a daily workout.* Perhaps a quantum physicist could pull this off, but I needed a different technique. I thought of the least productive hour of my day: the last one. The hour before bed belonged to the television, streaming movies. What if I chopped off that hour and grafted it onto the beginning of the next day? To put it simply, I would go to bed an hour earlier and wake up an hour early.

And I thought, *That sucks.* Sacrifice an hour of relaxation to get up before dawn? Did I have the Aristotelian courage to actually accomplish that? No, I did not. So I practiced a technique I had honed from many years of writing: I procrastinated. I waited until the following autumn, when on one November day the United States government granted us an extra hour. On that day, daylight saving time turned to standard time, and seven o'clock in the morning magically became six. Being married to a morning person, I was already in the habit of getting up at six, so now my wakeup time became five. Boom, there was my extra hour.

I stuck to that hour, even when daylight saving came around the following spring. The next year, I used the standard time change to set my clock back yet another hour. I was now getting up at four every morning! Late television time turned into early me time—a peaceful period when the phone stayed silent, no one texted, and the dawning world was my oyster.

Not that I used it wisely; not yet. While I had succeeded in carving out 8 percent of the twenty-four-hour cycle for exciting new habits, I remained unprepared to actually acquire those habits. The thought of doing anything useful at that godawful time of the . . . can you even call four o'clock morning? Writing, working out, reading improving books, whatever, seemed daunting. I lacked the courage to attempt them.

Still, I had the time. Eventually, I got used to having nothing else to do that early. So I chose to spend those two hours reading. Eventually, I began spending the second hour doing an easy downloaded workout. Over the months, that workout turned into harder workouts. My reading hour became a writing hour. It's not that I pushed myself to do any of these things. I just got a little bored with the easy way. The writing and workouts seemed novel and therefore somewhat attractive.

Plus, each small accomplishment added to my courage. Just look: I had managed to get up two hours earlier than my already early wakeup time! What's more, I did it seven days a week, even Sundays! I was so proud of this feat that I declared my own time zone, Jaylight saving. It was like any other time zone, and not an entirely crazy one. People who fly to London from New York don't think it especially odd to have to get up five hours earlier the next morning. We call the adjustment period jet lag, as if blaming it on the transportation. What the Greenwich Observatory did for the world's time zones I did for my very own schedule.

There was a downside, of course. Jaylight saving would have been perfect if more people than just my wife and I had been in it. Friends learned not to invite us to any dinner that began after five P.M. Still, I was willing to embrace that particular suck.

Besides, the benefits of those extra hours kept adding up. When it got light enough, I would head outside for brisk walks. The walks turned into runs, and the runs turned into trail runs, and eventually I was going up mountains in my home state of New Hampshire. That early in the morning, I was not tempted to eat junk, so I focused on nutrition drinks that wouldn't upset my stomach during workouts. I went from push-ups and pull-ups to workouts using dumbbells, and I got stronger. Those two hours of Jaylight saving transformed into an hour of writing followed by an hour of working out, and the writing hour—sheer coffee-enabled hard work, no matter how I framed it—turned the workouts into playtime, something I actually looked forward to.

You could justifiably hate me for telling you this. But I don't mean this story to show what great courage and self-discipline I had. In fact, the Tortoise Method and Jaylight saving let me carve out those good-habit hours without much bravery or discipline. My cumulative habits simply ratcheted themselves up.

> Exercise:
>
> 1. Set a goal and make it shiny. Consider a Hyperbole.
>
> 2. Carve out the time. Ideally, use the transition in the fall from daylight saving to standard time. Simply go

to bed and get up as if the time had never changed, gaining that extra hour in the morning.

3. Indulge yourself in that extra hour. It's yours to do whatever you want. Meanwhile, congratulate yourself. It took a bit of courage to do something as strange as exploiting the federal government's time standards.

4. Take that boost of courage and set a tiny new habit in that early hour. Read, practice a new skill, take an online lesson, or exercise. Whatever small thing leads to your goal, you now are courageous enough to try it.

5. Ratchet up. Celebrate each new habit, and once you get used to it, see if you can make it a tad more ambitious.

Habits turn extremes into norms. Benjamin Franklin practiced a morning routine of sitting naked by an open window even in the dead of winter. He thought it was good for him. Men and women scurrying to work in the early hours would doubtless notice this pale, plump figure in the window and consider the man to be a lunatic. But over the years, Franklin probably found it upsetting when he traveled and lacked an appropriate place for his air bath. I only remember that Jaylight saving comprises an extremely limited time zone when my friends learn about it. All they see is a guy who literally has no night life.

Each of us experiences a completely different reality. As the gorgeous rhetorician Gorgias knew, our sense of reality comes in part from the rhetorical devices that interpret it. Gain control of these all-important soul-bending devices and you can begin asserting the kind of reality that leads to ultimate happiness.

THE TOOLS

<u>Lure & Ramp.</u> Focus on the end delight, then chunk the means to achieve it.

<u>Tortoise Method.</u> While the name for this device comes from Aesop, not Aristotle (who loved Aesop's tales), the technique is purely Aristotelian. In his *Rhetoric,* the canny philosopher argued that to move an audience to action—the hardest trick of all—the persuader must stimulate desire for the goal, then convince the audience that the choice involves little pain or sacrifice. By breaking down the required actions into small steps, the audience can achieve that goal almost without thinking.

But Aristotle knew that the most ambitious achievements come from repeating those steps ad infinitum. He became history's most passionate advocate of habits—the single best way for a person to bring "the moving principle back to . . . the ruling part of himself." In other words, habits attach our actions to our noble soul. Aristotle said that virtue is little more than our habits.

10

Charms

Change the Voice in Your Head

The Forever Diamond and other reality benders

"Gorgias declares that nothing exists; and if anything exists it is unknowable; and if it exists and is knowable, yet it cannot be indicated to others."

—Aristotle, *On Melissus, Xenophanes, and Gorgias*

At this point you have gotten a look at some of rhetoric's most powerful self-persuasion tools. Each has the potential to bolster your courage and aim you toward some glorious goal. And yet, when I began my training for Mount Moosilauke, gasping up hills and forcing my Tin Man body into torturous yoga positions, I admit it: I began to doubt some of this rhetoric. The language in my head failed to match all those impressive rhetorical tools. How could I truly know, in light of my expanded waistline, my moments of sheer cowardice, the lies I had told my loved ones, that I was worthy?

Classical rhetoric gave me an answer. To be honest, it's a weird solution, but it has striking parallels with modern science. Some of the ancients would say that you and I need to strip our brains down and get rid of our reality for a moment. Gorgias—gold-statued Gorgias—claimed that reality is not really a thing at all. There is no reality. Nothing exists. At any rate, if anything did exist, it would not be knowable. And if something existed and was indeed knowable, we would be unable to share that knowledge with others. Gorgias reasoned that no one perceives the same reality or can agree on it. Everyone starts from a different perspective that represents a different world.

Neuroscience shows that the man has a point. Your brain has no direct connection to the world. It sits wetly in your skull, receiving signals from various inputs and creating a composite scene. It's very good at supplementing missing information with its own imagination. For instance, we all have a blind spot in each eye, where light signals get blocked by an optic nerve. Hold up a finger and close one eye, then the other, and the finger will appear to change position. The combination of those two spots creates a gap; on the Web you'll find experiments to make your finger disappear altogether. Your brain fills in that gap on its own, imagining a reality that it thinks should exist.

Gorgias took this notion a big step further. Because no one ever sees precisely the same thing, and so there's no consensus on what exists, he concluded that nothing is real. While this may sound like something Donald Sutherland would say in the *Animal House* pot-smoking scene, Gorgias had created a big Gorgian knot of logic. He argued that only rhetoric could untie it, by creating an impression of reality that allows us to share our known world. Just learn rhetoric—ideally by paying a Sophist a hefty tuition—and you can lead your fellow humans to that shared existence. Gorgias essentially patented reality. It was as if Ralph Lauren argued that the only clothing is Ralph Lauren–branded clothing; or as if Coca-Cola sued, claiming that no other liquid could count as a beverage; or as if I declared that chocolate ice cream is the only true dessert and that other kinds of "desserts" are just kidding. (Actually, I do believe that.)

Unfortunately for Gorgias's legacy, Aristotle came along and shot down that theory. While Aristotle's logic is unbeatable, I would not recommend reading his rebuttal without a supply of ibuprofen ("... for the objects of sight and hearing are for the reason that they are in each case cognized..."). Besides, Gorgias had a point, at least when it came to our perception of reality. Belief trumps facts in persuasion. Even Aristotle reluctantly came to that conclusion when he wrote his *Rhetoric*. Truth is one thing. Belief is another. And while, according to Aristotle's philosophy, not even eloquent Gorgias could change the truth, his rhetoric could influence what people perceived to be true. In persuading an audience, what you get them to believe is as good as the truth. This does not require bending reality. Aristotle came to realize that we need only to bend souls.

And, to my great relief, I discovered that some of rhetoric's soul-bending methods actually worked like magic.

The Magic of Holy Cows

Long before Gorgias and Aristotle, practitioners had been warping people's sense of reality by using magic charms. Certain words, uttered in a precise way, could produce mystical effects. We moderns still believe that, in a way. Some words can cast a spell so powerful that we're forbidden from saying them. Not long ago, uttering the word *bloody* among Brits could almost cause a riot; it referred to the blood of Christ, and so acted as a curse. Whole lexicons have developed around the avoidance of taking the Lord's name in vain. *Gee whiz* and *zounds* stand for "God's wounds." *Holy cow* equals "holy Christ." *Jeepers:* "Jesus's person." All these expressions attempt to work around an offense so great that it was listed third among the Ten Commandments in Jewish scripture. Invoking the name of a god—in this case, *the* God—could have terrible consequences. *Gosh darn*ing someone to *heck* could literally condemn someone to hell.

Other words could cast a more benign spell. The magi, mystical priests in ancient Persia, were masters of spells. They were not alone. Throughout Europe, Asia, and the Middle East, professional mystics printed incantations on lead tablets or amulets called charms; the word comes from the Latin *carmen,* meaning "song" or "incantation." Archaeologists continue to dig up charms today. These leaden expressions warded off evil spirits or enemies' curses. The texts were not the sort of empty-headed phrases we see on Valentine candy hearts; many of these ancient charms followed strict patterns, or rhythms, that helped work the magic.

Aristotle likewise understood that certain rhythms did more than just please the ear. The poets who first composed these patterns discovered that they induced a certain state in listeners. Rhythmic language could "express inanities," Aristotle wrote, and audiences would suck them up. That discovery led to Sophist proto-rap-stars like Gorgias adopting a poetic prose style to lull the masses into belief. Shakespeare, who learned rhetoric at the Stratford Grammar School, employed those rhythms in his plays. To lend gravitas to the more formal speeches, the ones uttered by nobles and tragic heroes, he used blank verse—iambic pentameter without rhymed endings: ba *dum*, ba *dum*, ba *dum*, ba *dum*, ba *dum*. To end a big speech with a bang, he used a rhyming couplet with the same rhythm. Here's Hamlet:

> *The time is out of joint, O cursed spite*
> *That ever I was born to set it right!*

It was the dramatic equivalent of a rim shot, words that not only punctuated a thought but drilled it into the audience's heads.

So, what does this have to do with making changes in your life? Ancient scholars parsed those rhythms and studied the ways that patterns of language and novel uses of words could affect audiences. They named the devices of this crafted speech *schema*, or schemes. The Romans called them *figura*: figures. To invoke *your* figurative magic, this chapter will show how to craft your own self-motivating charms. The psychological theory behind them harkens back to the original use of leaden charms. Figures—along with their cousins, the tropes—can turn hard into easy, the novice into an expert, and lame into heroic. Use them on yourself and you can work magic on your goals and habits.

Disclaimer: Getting used to even the most effective self-motivating figure will take some time. A fresh charm can seem as inane as a pop song lyric. (*Ooh, you make my motor run, my motor run / Got it comin' off of the line, Sharona.*) Consider a charm to be like a prescription medication; it needs time to take effect. You must repeat it to yourself like a Top 40 song on rotation until it turns from silly to natural to a universal truth. Modern neuroscientists have studied the effects of repetition on the brain; the research shows that charms actually work.

First, though, let's get to the most useful figure for changing ourselves.

The Candy-Coated War Cry

The orators in ancient Greece and Rome recognized the magic of rhythm. They noticed that the cadence of an expression could have a huge influence on an audience. Cicero was especially fond of one of the more powerful rhythms, the **paean**. We think of the paean today as a song or poem that praises, gives thanks, or celebrates a triumph. But it first meant words that heal. The original Paean was a Greek god who served as official physician to the immortals on Olympus. He became associated with language that warded off evil or injury. Soldiers would chant paeans as they went into battle, asking Apollo or Thanatos, the god of death, to spare them.

For maximum effect, a paean had to be expressed in prescribed rhythms. Cicero wrote that one kind of paean began with a long syllable followed by three short ones: *Stop doing it. Get on to it. Press down on it.* Another kind consisted of several short syllables: *Beaten them all; clatter of hooves.* Combine the two and you have a convincing spell. Given its ability to stir the blood, soldiers began using the paean as a rhythmic chant to gin up their courage as they marched into battle. They called this particular war cry paean a *slogan*.

While the rhythms in Greek and Latin seem foreign to us, our brains have changed little over the centuries. Cicero called the paean a "heroic" rhythm, quoting Homer's description of Apollo: *Golden-haired far-shooter, son of Zeus.* You could almost imagine classics majors chanting that in a basketball game. We can still find English versions of the slogan-style paean in the nerdy college football chant: *Repel them, repel them, make them relinquish the ball!* Activists are especially fond of the protest paean: *What do we want? Justice! When do we want it? Now!* And you can hear it in the empowering song: *Hit the road, Jack / Don't you come back no mo'!*

There must be a reason that the device pops up over the millennia, in languages around the world. The paean seems to make an excellent command: "Hey, you. Pay attention!" In some settings, it can come across as noble. And in our own capitalist economy, paeans worked their magic to foster whole industries.

Lay's potato chips: *Betcha can't eat just one.* This classic paean starts with three short syllables, then applies the brakes with three long ones. The hugely successful slogan seems creepy today, given America's addiction crisis—not to mention the snack food industry's deliberate approach to making its products addictive. With its Lay's potato chips, Frito-Lay actually bragged about it. One chip will get you hooked! Lay's, the gateway snack! When Pringles came along, its agency's copywriters saw a good thing in the competition. They came up with "Once you pop, you can't stop." This rhyming paean—three short syllables, then another three—tells consumers that popping the vacuum-sealed lid of a Pringles can opens a delightful Pandora's box of addiction. Do these slogans make all that much sense? No matter. Lay's sold $4 billion worth of unstoppable chips in 2023. Pringles took in $1.3 billion. Pure magic.

The New York Times: "All the News That's Fit to Print." Another paean. It also composes an isocolon—two equal clauses expressing opposite things—in balanced phrases: "All the news," then a "That's" for a fulcrum, followed by "fit to print." This worthy expression has stuck around since 1896, when it won a contest held by owner Adolph Ochs. The slogan beat some alliterative competition, including "News, Not Nausea" and "Fresh Facts Free from Filth." There's a lesson here. Mediocre writers often turn to alliteration when they feel desperate for a bit of wit. But alliteration is one of the weaker figurative elements. It can help you remember a concept, but not to believe in it. Rhythm and repetition have a more unconscious sticky effect. What's more, "All the News That's Fit to Print" arguably affected the company's entire ethos by implying that the *Times* was the newspaper of record, the first draft of history, encompassing all that was happening—minus the nauseating and filthy.

Nike: "Just Do It." The three short words employ sharp consonants, coming down hard on the action verb. It cuts Cicero's first kind of paean by skipping the last syllable; he probably would have preferred "Just Conquer It." But the slogan follows Aristotle's advice to make the first step of any enterprise seem easy. The *just* is a trigger. No thinking. Take the plunge. Marketing historians point to a grim origin for this slogan. Legendary ad executive Dan Wieden got the idea from the murderer Gary Gilmore, who in 1977 became the first person in ten years to be executed in this country. Gilmore faced his firing squad and said, "Let's do it." And so this murderous drifter coined three of the most famous last words. Wieden used it to craft the greatest command in advertising history.

Why spend all this time on the paean? And how on earth could you and I come up with the sort of war cry that earns brilliant marketing minds the big money? Granted, the best slogans are not easy to make. But with repetition, they can lubricate our habits and enforce belief in our goals. If a few rhythmic words can conjure up whole junk food empires, think what they can do for you and me.

One way to craft your own paean is to imitate an existing one. Take the M&Ms slogan with its Beethoven beat: *Melts in your mouth, not in your hand.* The short-short-short-long rhythm can serve as a reminder motto to keep you focused. An antithetical isocolon can also correct your form in any physical activity. I use this paean to adjust my terrible posture: *Head on a swivel, not in my lap.* For some reason (my unhealthy profession most likely), I look down when I walk or run, and my head tends to droop lower as I go. The slogan puts my head in the right place, both figuratively and literally. The antithesis—do this, not that—can be annoying. But the rhythm lets you bounce past the command and right into action.

The more traditional paean (*Golden-haired far-shooter, son of Zeus*) can push you past your natural inertia, especially first thing in the morning. Isaac Newton might as well have been thinking of my state of mind in the still-dark morning when he wrote his First Law of Thermodynamics. An object at rest (me) tends to stay at rest (in bed). These days, habit alone gets me up. But a good old-fashioned paean can jump-start the habit. Back when getting up at four in the morning seemed ridiculously masochistic, I would answer the alarm by muttering: *Just one foot, on the floor, then stand up!* You can recite your paean aloud in a singsong voice, or silently in your head if there are witnesses. No, it does not have to inspire. It need not be pretty. Nor—and this is the beauty of it—does it even have to make much sense.

A paean can also help improve an eating habit. *First the nutrition, then the junk.* Note how this goes beyond the rhythm of the get-out-of-bed paean. The "then" sets up a sequence that, combined with the rhythm, begins to seem inevitable after you repeat it a few thousand times.

If you feel up to it, try ginning up some paean-esque slogans of your own. Use the Beethoven beat, short-short-short-long. Maybe craft an antithesis (*Do it like a hero, not like a chump!*). Think about a habit you struggle to stick with and use a paean as a kind of motivational glue. Or craft a paean that focuses on the consequences. *Booze makes me miserable, think of the mor-ning!* And don't try to make your slogan poetic or even literate. It will sound natural once you develop a habit of repeating it. Then give it time. Let the charm work its magic.

Pump Up Your Ventromedial Prefrontal Cortex!

Advertisers, along with social mavens, know that language alone won't cut it. To get consumers to buy, or voters to vote, or your own unmotivated self to act, even the best slogans have to be repeated again and again and again. Redundancy makes the world go round . . . and round. This helps explain why the inanities Aristotle complained about work so well. The point of a paean or other slogan is not to change one's opinion. "Why, a diamond *is* forever! How true! I shall take out a disastrously large bank loan and secure my lover for eternity!" Or: "Look at that child on TV enjoying tomato soup! That Campbell's Soup must certainly be good!" Slogans don't change minds. They bend souls—creating unshakable belief in your own goals and actions—through the repeated hammer blows of **repetition.**

To put it scientifically, repetition literally changes minds, by building and strengthening neural connections. When you repeat a slogan to yourself, you activate the ventromedial prefrontal cortex—the part of your brain that interprets reality. The more you repeat an expression, the stronger the associated synapses become, reinforcing a view of the world. In this sense, Gorgias was right: Reality exists in our internal impression of our surroundings. Our perception comes down to the electrochemical signals that zoom back and forth between neurons in the prefrontal cortex. This part of the brain also happens to control the amygdala—the primitive fight-or-flight section—automating our actions. The more we repeat a choice or an attitude, whether it has to do with morning routines or potato chips, the more we change our minds.

Over time, slogans certainly alter the structure of our brains. In bolstering the connections between neurons—a process of learning and memory that neurologists call long-term potentiation—repetition increases the efficiency of communication about a concept while strengthening the ties between that concept and your own identity. As Aristotle would put it, repeating a slogan ties a particular reality to your soul. Eventually, that reality becomes part of what psychologists call your implicit memory, an unconscious sense of things. You need not think that a diamond is forever. With enough repetition, diamonds become associated with eternal commitment.

Weirdly, brain studies seem to show that the practice of repeating words or actions actually improves neuroplasticity, the ability to retain things in your brain. The more you memorize, the better you are at memorizing. Also, the more you practice the piano, the better you might be at perfecting a pickleball serve. Repeat a slogan to yourself and you might become more adept at absorbing, and believing in, other helpful slogans. All of this leads to belief in your own improbable goals. Repeating an action makes it a habit. Repeating the habit in turn releases endorphins and other feel-good chemicals in the brain.

Sorry about all this repetition, but I hope you see the value. Repetition makes perfect. It's one secret to self-persuasion.

Serenading the Dancing Cockroach

While my paeans made me want to repeat them more, in the long run, the benefit of these expressions lay in the repetition itself. I'm a little embarrassed to tell you what those expressions were. When

I first started saying them to myself, they made me smile just because they were so silly. Over time, though, they became slices of my own personal reality.

To recover from my hip problem, I had to force myself to perform painful mobility exercises, and then hold even more agonizing yoga poses. I have nothing against yoga—some of my best friends, et cetera—but whoever invented those vinyasa exercises seemed to have had a mean sense of humor. Downward dog? Happy baby? *Dancing cockroach?* Never mind the humiliating names. The poses themselves seem designed specifically to make us fart. After sweating in the back row behind dozens of lissome sprites, I switched to grunting in front of yoga videos. No, not grunting. You're not supposed to grunt in yoga. So I created a yoga-enabling paean to play silently in my head:

Breathe in, breathe in, hold yourself happy and still.

If you saw my face when I first started mutely reciting this paean, you would not see happy and still. But after a few hundred repetitions, I could almost hear a calm voice whispering to my own serene soul.

No, I don't expect you to believe me. I certainly wouldn't. If only I could somehow magick you into reading that last passage a thousand times, you would want to create a paean of your own.

Many years ago, when I got promoted to my first management job, my mother gave me an empowering teddy bear. It came dressed in a three-piece suit and contained a half-dozen raspy recordings. Pull Teddy's string and it would say things like "You're on the way to the top!" "There's nothing you can't do!" "You're a winner! Teddy knows." When Mom gave me that thing, I felt a little hurt. Did she think I was so emotionally unprepared for leadership that I needed a support stuffed animal? I don't know, maybe she meant it as a joke, or simply thought the bear was a goofy way of expressing her pride in me. But during the first year in my new role, I confess I pulled that string countless times. And it helped. Over time, it stopped seeming silly. I *was* a winner. Teddy knew.

So it was with my breathy yoga mantra. Thanks to weeks of therapy and exercises, I found myself walking without a limp. Soon, I could run, slowly, without much pain. But, to run my age up Mount Moosilauke, I had to do much better than that. Running has a strangely consistent mathematics. No matter what length or speed the event, your feet should hit the ground at 180 beats per minute. Competitive marathoners, sprinters, trail runners, hurdlers, even pole vaulters all maintain that three-strikes-per-second rhythm. While you can download a playlist with 180 bpm songs—Billy Idol's "Dancing with Myself," Rihanna's "Umbrella"—I found that a bouncy paean could serve a double purpose of speed and motivation.

Quickening, quickening, feet barely touching the ground!

Actually, while my feet definitely sped up, I never did achieve a 180 bpm gait. And when I resumed running up northern New England's steep, rocky trails, I found the need for a different paean—one that could help me reframe those slippery boulders.

My legs love rocks, I flow up rocks!

And then I even came up with a paean to get me out of bed in the morning. For more than a decade, I've used it every day—including this one. When the alarm goes off, I whisper to myself:

Make this a glorious day.

And, ever so subtly, without my even being fully aware, it already is.

Tropical Soul Benders

Rhythmic expressions, repeated over and over, can shift your mood, your feeling of what is hard, and even your own sense of self. But to go full Gorgias on ourselves, creating our own reality, we need even more powerful weapons: the tropes.

These rhetorical soul benders turn political squabbles into wars on the middle class, body parts into tests of character, and individuals into gods or villains. Film reviewers often refer to movie tropes—the supportive Black friend, or the carnal locomotive entering a tunnel. Political pundits pronounce as a trope the "weaponizing" of abortion or drag shows. All this may sound confusing; but once we see the tropes in all their naked glory, they will help us shift our own reality.

The word *trope* derives from the Greek *tropos,* "a turning." A heliotropic plant turns itself to face the sun. The tropics are the regions of the earth that, like the cheery plant, turn toward the sun. Then there's the troposphere: the lowest layer of the atmosphere, where the wind twists and turns.

The Greeks had even richer uses for the term. Homer's epithet for Odysseus, the man who traveled on the original odyssey, was *polytropos*. It literally means "one of many turnings." To keep readers from throwing the book in despair, translators have changed that to "a complicated man," "the wily one," "a crafty man," "a versatile man," "a cunning man," and "a man of twists and turns." This last one, by Robert Fagels in a 1996 translation, comes closest to the meaning, because *polytropos* is a pun. After Odysseus helped wreck the city of Troy, he took an extremely roundabout journey home to his island kingdom of Ithaca. The sea god Poseidon bore a grudge against the hero and forced the journey into an almost endless round of unexpected turns and plot twists on his way back to his wife, son, and cattle.

But the epithet was not just travel based. While Odysseus had the right stuff of a Marvel-level superhero—sexy athleticism, noble birth, uncanny war-fighting skills—his superpower was the gift of gab. The man was the most persuasive mortal in all the Greek myths. He was one tricky hombre, a master of the artful dodge. With just his words he could turn the mind and bend the soul. He inspired his men, talked sulking Achilles into joining battle, tricked the giant Cyclops, and fooled his own wife into thinking he was a homeless man. Every time the gods threw a barrier in his way, Odysseus wormed around it. His story eventually became a trope; today we often call a complicated career or difficult feat an odyssey. The word adds special effects to our life story.

In fact, a trope acts like a James Cameron movie. When we go to a theater, we prepare ourselves to suspend disbelief. We choose to think that the tall blue humanoids on the screen are inhabitants of the exo-moon Pandora and not actors with dots on their faces reciting lines in front of a green screen. No one leaves the theater with plans to mine the planet's valuable unobtanium. Much more sneakily, a trope like metonymy ("the suits in the C-suite") or synecdoche ("She's such a Karen") do much of their magic without anyone noticing the manipulation.

Aristotle called this kind of wordplay "analogical" thinking, and he spent many pages trying to explain it. An analogy, he wrote, finds similar traits in two different things. The philosopher knew that many animals practice this kind of thinking. A wolf detects a delectable scent in the mud and immediately thinks, *rabbit*. The mud is no rabbit, but it emits a rabbity perfume. The wolf runs around seeking more analogies. (Sherlock Holmes would call them clues; inductive reasoning is a kind of analogical thinking.) A deep track in the mud denotes a big, juicy rabbit. If the left footprint looks shallower than the right one, then the clever wolf understands that her prey is limping.

We humans evolved to take analogical thinking a good deal further. We turned analogy into a cluster of calculation, including extrapolation, symbolizing, and generalizing. Over the millennia, our rhetoric evolved beyond one-to-one relationships between like things. While a wolf smells rabbit and thinks "rabbit," we hear a politician and think, "I smell a liar." Like Odysseus, we became polytropic. And our analogies bloomed from trope to trope.

Metaphor: Fight On, Topiary Man

Tropes serve as language's actors, playing pretend. They begin with Aristotle's analogies and then distort reality to make relatable things seem the same. If you look at a politician's lush, perfectly shaped hair and think it looks like topiary, then you're employing an analogy. *This head is like topiary.* Now, if you're immature and mean and have some Photoshop skill, you can transform his head into an anthropomorphic bush. That's a metaphor. You pretend that the head is not just *like* topiary, it's literally an artistic hedge.

Metaphors help us dramatize our own lives, turning the mundane into the cinematic. Our competitive, meaningless jobs are a rat race. The spouse we come home to every night is an angel or, heaven forbid, a ball and chain. A robocall makes our blood boil. All these thoughts and expressions play pretend, turning analogies into ersatz reality.

The word *metaphor* comes from the Greek, meaning "to carry

over." A metaphor borrows a characteristic from one thing and pretends to be another thing. They can be downright head-turning. Aristotle said that the trope "puts the subject before our eyes." It makes us look at a recovering alcoholic and see a heroic voyager; we gaze upon a presidential candidate and witness botanical art. The philosopher believed that a great metaphor should have the startling combination of antithesis and vividness. The more unlike the two objects seem to be, and the more memorable the picture that results, the better the metaphor. Aristotle especially admired a metaphor coined by the Greek author Aesion. Recounting how Athens conquered Sicily and turned it into a mirror-image colony, Aesion wrote: "The Athenians poured the city into Sicily." Not a bad metaphor at all.

Metaphor, the simplest trope of all, fuels more feel-good song lyrics than any other. ("Fuels": another metaphor.) When R. Kelly sings, "I believe I can touch the sky," he's not necessarily under the influence of a hallucinogen but rather capturing (to use a metaphor) a soaring ambition. Queen's "We Are the Champions" turns a rock band into war heroes who "keep on fighting till the end"; the aforementioned end, presumably, is not death but a Grammy.

> Exercise: Craft a metaphor of your very own. Instead of promising yourself to go for a jog, you can plan an escape. It's the exact same jog, only with a more attractive label. Grading student papers can become—what? Playing professional cultural critic or literary editor? Fine-tuning young characters?

All this may seem laughable (which, at least, can cognitively ease your mood), but metaphors can exert a powerful placebo effect. A woman says of her morning workout, "This is my coffee," and part of her brain enacts a stimulant. Most of us think of our coffee as coffee, not a metaphor. But tropes, like laughter, often make the best medicine.

Irony: Stephen Colbert's Sharp Dullness

Only word experts and extreme geeks consider irony a trope. It seems nothing like a metaphor. But if you think of tropes as actors playing pretend, irony counts as the most thespian of all. Characters who play against type—think Stephen Colbert in his fake-conservative days—are being ironic. A sarcastic teenager bleating, "Niiiiice!" at a tray-dropping classmate in the cafeteria practices a crude form of irony, sounding encouraging while projecting the opposite meaning. Southerners have turned "Bless her heart" into an insult, ironically damning through faint praise.

The word *irony* comes from, wait for it, the ancient Greek. It means "a sharp dullness." Irony creates a kind of truth duet: two meanings ringing simultaneously. You can find this in your own backyard. A gentle butterfly has a pattern on its wings that makes it look like a fierce predator. Totally ironic. An innocent-looking Venus flytrap offers its sweet nectar to insects, only to eat its victims, thus forming its own ironic Little Shop of Horrors. Nature is full of these Janus-like two-way feints and head fakes.

The same holds for our social and public lives. A scornful citizen speaks up at a town council meeting and says, "With all the respect that's due you . . ." She's practicing an ironic figure called *adianoeta:* saying one thing while meaning the exact opposite.

Usually, the trope works best when you have both a victim (town councilor) and an audience (citizens) who detect separate meanings. Irony can serve as a kind of code known only to those who "get it." This can make for a cruel trope. So, what possible use would it have in self-persuasion? How can irony even work if you're both audience and victim?

Truth be told, I originally thought that irony would be the least useful trope for self-persuasion. But I gained new respect for irony when I began experimenting with rhetorical devices on myself. The effort can seem ridiculous; it's easy to see right through to your own manipulation. Irony can ease that feeling. Some of these mantras I said to myself seemed at first like those cheesy old self-affirmations that came on tapes you could play in your car. "I am a worthy person, capable of great things." You're kidding, right? But I found that if I leaned into the humor and could recite a slogan with a bit of a smile, my brain softened slightly, opening up a crack to belief. Repeat the thing often enough, and it stops seeming ironic.

When I began talking myself into doing early-morning workouts, my wife would ask me afterward how they went. I would stand before her, sweaty and sore, and say, "Refreshing!" Which was ironic and made me smile. But when this became a routine between us—"How was it?" "Refreshing!"—a part of me began to believe unironically that working out was not entirely horrible. Irony's sharp dullness turned shiny.

And so the meanest trope, the one that victimizes the clueless with its secret codes, became a useful way to persuade myself. You might keep this in mind as you progress through this book. You will come across devices that make you cringe. Irony can get you past the cringing.

Metonymy: Your Own Private Labrador

Irony can help us embark (nautical metaphor) on a great new venture. But what venture are we supposed to be starting? When it comes to sorting through the chaos in our lives and finding opportunistic openings, one trope can serve as a door opener. Metonymy can be the most difficult to understand. But if you master this weird little device, the world might suddenly open up to interesting opportunities.

Metonymy enacts a marriage between two or more things that share a kind of chemistry. The metaphor does this as well, but the metonymy turns the chemistry itself into an object or action. Red is a color, and it's the color of your hair, so I'll call you Red. Whiskey is held in bottles, and I've been drinking a lot of whiskey, so my friend notices I've been *hitting the bottle*. What I'm hitting—drinking, actually—is not the glass itself but the contents. Well-dressed businessmen wear suits, so we'll call the men suits. This is why rhetoricians call metonymy the trope of contiguity—the state of things bordering each other. If they share a trait or a container or an action, you can turn them into a metonymy.

Applying the rhetorical perspective to technology, we can say that the iPhone is metonymic. Steve Jobs married the cellphone with the iPod, two gadgets that shared listening and portability. He added the digital camera, which shared with the iPod the ability to store and organize files. Admittedly, he probably did not say to himself, "I'm going to create a metonymic device!" But that's what the iPhone is . . . metonymic. Similarly, Lin-Manuel Miranda probably was not thinking of a metonymy when he read a biography of the brash, wildly ambitious, improvisational Alexander Hamilton and combined his story with brash, improvisational hip-hop music. Both Jobs and Miranda may have inherited a combinational intuition at the genetic level. The rest of us mortals can use the trope to create marriages of opportunity on our own.

One way to construct a metonymy is to describe an occasion in the simplest possible terms. Pidgin dialects, which merge languages to allow contiguous cultures to communicate, do just that. Nigerian pidgin uses "How body?" for "How are you doing?" Instead of "Don't be angry," the dialect says, "Make you no vex," a nice way of implying that emotions are self-created. "Why strong face?" tells someone to relax. Some pidgin expressions can get elaborate. I once heard a New Guinea pidgin description of a piano as "big black box hit him in teeth he cry," and of an elevator as "room go up belly down."

Pidgin thinking simplifies everything to the point where you realize that much of what we see around us consists of combinations. Clarence Birdseye, inventor of flash-frozen foods, seems to have been blessed with a pidgin mind. A naturalist and fur trader, he accepted an invitation by a band of Inuit to go ice fishing in Labrador, within the Arctic Circle. They drilled a hole in the ice and helped him lower a baited line. The temperature had dipped to twenty below zero. Within minutes, Birdseye felt a tug on the line. He hauled against it and slowly brought up a jerking burden that almost instantly turned into a dead weight. His companions helped him pull it onto the ice: a thoroughly frozen Arctic char. That evening, the group cooked the fish. To Birdseye's delight, it tasted perfectly fresh.

Birdseye then seems to have experienced a metonymic eureka moment. He fished. He pulled up food that never rots. The world certainly could use food that never rots. And he thought: *How can I make my own personal Labrador?* Back home in Massachusetts, he pulled together a few blocks of ice, some salt brine, and an electric fan, for a total expense of seven dollars. After revising the method (and going through bankruptcy) he sold his frozen-fish company in 1929 for more than $23 million.

Clarence Birdseye pulled up a fish and imagined an industry. He brought the Arctic down, and suddenly Massachusetts virtually relocated to just south of the border with Labrador. Today, the frozen food industry in America alone is worth some $60 billion.

The kind of metonymic, pidgin-powered cognition that Birdseye applied to fish can help the rest of us. A friend of mine graduated from an Ivy League university wanting nothing more than to earn a modest living as a jeweler. She loved working with metal, heating things up and joining them together, making stones fit permanently into their settings. She found a jeweler willing to take her on as an apprentice for a low wage. Alex loved the work and proved herself extremely talented. But there was a problem: Jewelers are more than plentiful here in New England. The competition was too great to guarantee a successful business of her own; and despite her skill, no one wanted to hire her for decent pay.

One day Alex came home to her shabby apartment to find that the toilet she shared with a roommate had mysteriously stopped working. The landlord refused to fix it, saying that, for the crummy rent they were paying, he couldn't afford a plumber. Instead of complaining to the authorities, Alex went to work. An hour later, thanks to some ingenious plumbing, the toilet was fixed and peace reigned in the apartment. Still, Alex's life remained chaotic. What else was going to break down? How could she afford a normal life?

At this point, Alex began thinking metonymically, breaking down a complex situation into one plus one. Her process can work for us as well.

First, **find the essential elements.** A piano is a box with teeth that make noise. An elevator is a small room. Labrador is a freezer. Alex realized she wasn't just a barely employed jeweler. She was a *fixer*. She actually enjoyed repairing that toilet. Not that she wanted to become a plumber. She was a jeweler.

Next, **explore contiguities.** What seemingly unlike things could actually belong together? Plumbing entails clever ways to let water flow through pipes without leaking. This in turn requires the repairer to understand joints and fixtures. Why was Alex instantly good at understanding this stuff? Because making jewelry employed some of the same skills.

Finally, **look for the opening** in the chaos. Alex was blocked by a surplus of jewelers making jewelry. But jewelry, like toilets, can break. A woman with a loose diamond on her engagement ring is not about to let that slide. Alex wondered how many repair jewelers worked in New England. This created her eureka moment: As with plumbers, repair jewelers—those who specialize in broken jewelry—were in short supply. Alex loved working with metal, she enjoyed fixing things, there was a demand for skilled jewelers to fix jewelry, and she needed money. "I'm a plumber for broken jewels," she told me, using a perfect metonymy.

Besides inspiring an entire career, the metonymy can help us overcome the anxiety we feel about the success of others. Taylor Swift seems to have triggered an epidemic of what psychologists call Celebrity Worship Syndrome: a feeling of inadequacy that comes from comparing ourselves with famous accomplished people. How could anyone possibly measure up to this woman? She not only writes her own songs, plays her own guitar and piano, and owns her music; she also runs her own company and makes savvy billionaire-level investments. You don't have to be a Swiftie, or even enjoy her music, to feel a bit of CWS at the news that heads of state around the world are begging her to perform in their home countries to boost their economies. You and I will never be Taylor Swift.

Personally, I don't terribly mind not being her. The thought of wearing a sequin bathing suit in a packed arena gives me nightmares. But I get CWS whenever I read books by writers who are much more accomplished than I'll ever be.

Metonymy offers a cure. Focus on a slice of the character, not the whole thing. So you will never sing as well as Taylor. Could you write autobiographical lyrics? Or aim at her work ethic? She famously trained for her Eras tour by singing all forty-four songs while jogging on a treadmill. That turned into an extreme workout that endurance athletes across the land hyperbolically attempted. You won't want to turn the sound up on their online videos. The singing is hilariously awful. But that's not the point. The point is to take the best of Taylor that fits your own skills and desires.

What's your chaos that you'd like to change? Can you simplify its elements to the pidgin-level essentials? See any potential contiguities, any traits in an admirable person you might enhance in yourself? If not yet, no worries. Metonymies are hard. But having read this far, you may find yourself beginning to think rhetorically.

Synecdoche: A Most Delicious Rock

We've met Aristotle's technique of chunking a daunting goal into doable actions. There's a trope that makes the effort even easier. The synecdoche takes a sample of something and makes it represent the whole thing. (It can also do the opposite, but for self-persuasion purposes we'll stick to taking a piece of the whole.) When George W. Bush promised "boots on the ground" in Iraq, he was recruiting a synecdoche. The U.S. Army was not about to dump boots out of helicopters. "Boots on the ground" represented combat troops. The trope made a policy sound immediately active and the war in Iraq seem simple and doable.

Feel free to plagiarize Bush's speechwriters and turn a jog into "shoes on the street." It may not talk you into going for a run, but it's good trope practice. Gym bros use a similar synecdoche for a notoriously hard workout of barbell squats, lunges, Romanian deadlifts, and other forms of self-torture. They call it leg day. A cluster of painful activities focuses on a single leg. For most of these bros, leg day comprises two legs. But "legs day" would not make a synecdoche.

The trope is ideal for when you contemplate starting something. Call it the Stone Soup Method. Do you know this story? Several hungry strangers show up in a village carrying a big pot. They ask for food to cook, but the stingy villagers refuse. So the strangers calmly fill the pot with water, light a fire under it, and ostentatiously drop in a big stone. A villager asks, "What are you doing?"

"Making stone soup," one of the strangers replies. "It's delicious! We'll give you some, but it could use a bit of garnish." The villager offers a few carrots, and these get dropped in. Another villager comes by, and the strangers note that the soup could still use some potatoes. More villagers show up, and the garnishes become all kinds of vegetables, meat, and delectables. At last the stone soup is done, and the whole village feasts on what they think is a free meal. The tale has been told all over Europe, with variations substituting a nail, a button, and even an axe for the stone. Each version pretends that one small ingredient—stone, axe—comprises the whole meal. A one-pot synecdoche.

The same device can help you focus on the first step of any project, making it seem like the whole thing. A friend of mine has talked himself into cooking for his family every night by calling it "chopping." He likes to chop vegetables, so the tiresome additional steps of choosing meals, reading recipes, sautéing and stirring and all the rest, become, simply, chopping.

I like to sit in the early morning, so writing is sitting. You, on the other hand, may prefer the outdoors. So, to get yourself into the habit of running, you put on your running gear and go outside. As you head out into the frosty dawn, you say to your soul: "I want to see more and warm myself up." You might as well move your feet. For me, sitting is the stone of my soup. For, you, going outside may be the stone. Moving your feet just adds a garnish.

You can see that the meaning of words, and the different perspectives to them, can change your attitudes and actions. Charms and incantations—especially the singsong paean—can get you out of bed and pull you into better habits. Tropes can bend your sense of reality. Repeat them enough, and your soul may just be starting to bend to your will.

THE TOOLS

<u>Paean.</u> A rhythmic chant. *Push 'em back, shove 'em back, waaaaayyyy, back!* Come up with your own, repeat it often enough, and it can become your personal war cry.

<u>Repetition.</u> Repeat an expression often enough and it forms a virtual reality. If Gorgias knew about modern brain biology, he might argue that synaptic connections *are* reality—each person's very own slice of the universe. A charm that seems silly and illogical can turn into an absolute truth. Experiment with one that helps you reset a habit.

<u>Metaphor.</u> This Ur-trope pretends that one thing (golf resort) is another (heaven).

<u>Metonymy</u> takes people or things that share something—a container or trait or action—and makes that sharing the thing itself. The executive branch of the government is centered in a white building, so we'll call the presidency

the White House. Cities comprise athletic teams, so we'll say that Dallas beat Washington. Corpses have stiffened with rigor mortis, so we'll crassly metonymize them into "stiffs."

<u>Synecdoche</u> takes a sample (feet on the floor) and makes it represent an entirety (getting up early).

<u>Pidgin thinking</u>. Find the essential elements, explore contiguities, and look for an opening. The result is an inspirational metonymy.

11

Narrative

Tell Your Story

Aristotle's enchanting knots

"Spoken sounds are symbols of affections in the soul, and written marks symbols of spoken sounds."

—Aristotle, *On Interpretation*

Born storytellers can recount their terrible commute or boring meeting and still hold our rapt attention. The rest of humanity tells stories of the and-then variety: *We drove to Boston, the traffic was awful, then we parked in the hotel garage and checked in. And then we went shopping in Back Bay . . .* This narrative device (to use a flattering term) works perfectly well for court testimony but not so much for holding an audience on the edge of their seats. Well, so what? We're not all entertainers.

There are a couple reasons why the skill of telling a good yarn can help us personally. You've known skilled storytellers. Even the least trustworthy among them grab people's attention. And even when you're not supposed to be telling a story per se—giving a presentation or a lecture or a simple here's-to-the-couple wedding toast—a good grasp of narrative technique will make everything memorable, including your approaches to change. Telling a good story about yourself makes you memorable—including to yourself. After all, achieving a Hyperbole is a heroic act that requires a heroic character.

Besides, every great character, from Anna Karenina to Iron Man, *has* a story. When we encounter a mysterious person—someone with an unusual accent or interesting gait, or who's escorted by a pair of scary bodyguards—we ask, "What's her story?" We want to know the sequence of connected events that define the character we see before us. And storytelling can help you define your own character—not just for others, but for yourself as well.

"A sequence of connected events." That is the definition Aristotle gives for a plot. In his *Poetics,* he writes that connections make the story; one thing leads believably to another. And he means more than those and-then connections. We need to believe that each event *causes* the next one. When those events consist of the character's own actions, then the plot reveals that person's soul.

This leads to the second reason why we should improve our storytelling. The better the narrative, the more believable the character. Tell a heroic story, and we create a hero. If that story reflects your own heroic soul, then you begin to believe in it.

Story begets belief. We're more compelled by anecdotes than by statistics. A little girl gets rescued from a well, and suddenly every well seems a safety hazard. If you want perfect accuracy, you can commission a study and delve into the statistics of people falling into wells. Good luck making the evening news. To improve well safety, you should tell the story of that one little girl. In fact,

Aristotle said that, if you construct a compelling plot, the facts don't even have to be true. It doesn't matter if the kid never fell into the well at all; she can be a fiction. The story brings belief.

The Pizza Connection

We can see the power of narrative in politics. Stories compel people to fall for even the most bizarre fabrication. Imagine anyone believing that a Washington, D.C., pizzeria named Comet Ping Pong hosted a pedophile ring run by Hillary Clinton and her cronies. Yet the story, spread by online extremists, caught on. It evolved to the point where gullible people began believing that millions of girls and boys were being trafficked for sex. The reality, while sad, is less sensational. According to the Save the Children organization, some one hundred thousand to three hundred thousand children are being trafficked in this country. The term refers not just to sex but to other kinds of exploitation, including forced labor. Most traffickers are friends or relatives of the children's families. The real story is less dramatic than the one being bruited about, and the true one lacks a pedo pizzeria. But do the facts matter? A story, made from a plot of connected events, even untrue ones, will trump any data.

This is just more proof of what Aristotle called our "sorry human nature." But if we can master storytelling techniques, we can control belief—not just among online audiences but in ourselves. Besides stimulating faith in yourself, when you connect events that have yet to happen, you just might find belief in your own glorious future.

The connections make the story. So, what do I (and by "I" I mean Aristotle) intend by "connections"? Consider this example. We watch a movie where a character walks through a dry pasture. He looks behind him and sees a wall of fire. If nothing explained the fire, then Aristotle would leave the theater. The filmmaker failed to connect man and blaze. On the other hand, if in the previous shot the man had stopped, lighted a cigarette, and dropped the match, then the match would have linked the two. The fire would seem likely, even inevitable. The lit match makes the connection.

The character himself can connect one event to the next. We learn elsewhere in the movie that the man is the careless type, failing to water his horse. Maybe he's walking because he managed to lose his mount; we would then see the dropped match as the sort of thing the idiot would do.

At the same time, his actions let us know what kind of soul he has. Does he panic? Does he act resourcefully, cleverly finding a buffalo wallow and covering himself in mud? Or does he selflessly run back through the fire to warn the village?

The right story links can turn a boring character into an interesting one. Luke Skywalker is your typical teenage boy stuck on the farm while yearning to become a pilot for the empire. His dusty beige clothing and blond hair reflect a plain vanilla character. But his military ambition makes the link between meeting old Ben Kenobi and refusing to join the rebellion. Suppose he changed his mind an hour later (*Oh, what the heck, I might as well trust the Force*); then we would lose the plot. It would lack the connection. Instead, the movie has him come home to discover that the empire has murdered his only relatives. That event connects Luke to the events that follow. His responses turn him from farm boy to hero.

Knotty Tie Fighting

To some degree we are all Luke Skywalkers. Without soul-testing plot twists, our own characters can seem plain. Aristotle encourages us to bend our vanilla souls, adding irresistible flavor through events, using our own character as the connection. Through personal storytelling, we can make our character seem compelling enough to be worth all the effort to accomplish our goals. We want to give that interesting character a happy ending.

In his *Poetics*—a book that launched a thousand motion pictures—Aristotle describes the episodes in a story as a series of complications and resolutions, of "**tying**" (*desis*) and "**untying**" (*lusis*). Think of these as **event connections**. The character gets tangled in a problem. He tries to untangle himself, which leads to another knotty problem, and so on. The tying and untying form the connections between episodes and make the character himself more interesting.

To show how event connections can help make a goal seem inevitable, take my own vanilla self. Suppose someone wanted to know why I write for a living. Besides admitting that I can't handle tools and have no business sense, I could tell my story through the plain vanilla and-then narrative:

> In third grade I told my teacher, Mrs. Lord, that I wanted to be a writer. She suggested keeping a diary. I ran home and asked my mother for a notebook and pen. Then I wrote down my name. Then gradually I began to write different things. And then, over time, I wrote enough to think of myself as a writer.

Everything in this narrative is true, though I doubt anyone who read that passage would think that its author had the right ambition. Some writer he turned out to be. Instead, I should get Aristotelian and put in some connections—the episodes that tie and untie:

In third grade I told my teacher, Mrs. Lord, that I wanted to be a writer. "Writers write every day," she said. "You should keep a diary."

I said, "I can't keep a diary. I'm a boy. Boys don't have diaries." (*Tie*)

"Keep a journal, then." (*Untie*)

So I ran home and asked my mother for a notebook and pen. But when I sat down to write, I had no clue what to write about. (*Tie*) Next day, I asked Mrs. Lord what to do.

"Write about yourself," she said. (*Untie*)

After school that afternoon, I sat down again, determined to write about myself. The problem was, I was a normal boy in a normal suburb of Philadelphia in normal 1963. (*Tie*) Everything around me was less interesting than my comic books. *I was uninteresting*. So I wrote down my name, got up sadly, and played with my plastic soldiers. Still, writers write every day, so after school each day I sat down to write about myself, trying to find something—*anything*—interesting about myself to write.

After a couple of discouraging weeks, I overheard one of the teachers utter a profound philosophical statement: "You are what you eat." Eureka! (*Untie*) If I was what I ate, and keeping a journal meant writing about myself, then I could write what I had for lunch each day. That afternoon, I sat down and wrote myself for the ages: *Baloney sandwich and milk.*

The next day I did the same thing, writing down what I had for lunch: *Baloney sandwich and milk*. And I remembered that I ate the same lunch every day, even on weekends. (*Tie*) Still, I kept at my journal, wondering how this would make me a writer.

A classmate named Woody Woodward saved me. At lunch in the cafeteria, he balanced an open half-pint carton of milk on his head and it spilled, sending a marvelous white cascade down his face, which of course was hilarious. (*Untie*) When I wrote in my journal that afternoon, I discovered context. I was more than what I ate; I was what I experienced, and how I felt about that experience while I ate.

I called my journal *Lunch* and have been keeping it daily for the past sixty years.

That second account, while a good deal wordier than the first, and-then version, reveals a character who unfolds through a series of Aristotelian *episodes*. (The word originally referred to the action—the tying and untying—in a Greek tragedy that took place between choruses.) My first version tells a vanilla story with a vanilla character. The second shows a little boy untying problems in the quest for his writerly soul. Both stories are entirely true. But which character seems more compelling, even truer?

Narrative tools make persuasion more palatable. Episodes, well connected through likely or inevitable progressions, make the character himself more believable. This is why it helps to tell a story. You can play the hero of your life's tale if you make it a good one. That heroism in turn can put you into the persuadable state of cognitive ease, allowing you to convince yourself that you're capable of the seemingly impossible.

Even better, a good self-yarn can predict the future. All you have to do is make it come true.

The Heroic Space Farmer

Aristotle's theory of connections can help us use the plot structure that gets taught in schools: the **hero's journey**. This kind of story begins with the protagonist in his or her familiar world; say, the planet Tatooine. Some event—an aunt and uncle's murder—forces the hero out of this world and sends him on his empire-resisting quest. Along the way, he faces a series of obstacles and reaches a point of almost certain defeat (Darth Vader, Death Star), joins forces with some allies, and triumphs in the end. Each scene (or episode, as Aristotle and George Lucas would call it) leads to the next one, as the hero unties one problem only to face another. Eventually he learns a valuable secret or a bit of wisdom he can share when he returns home. Even better, he learns something important about himself (The value of staying on target? Luke's dark-side genetic inheritance?). Fade to black.

A high school student who uses the hero's journey for her college admissions essay can improve her chance of getting into her chosen school. Suppose she decides to write about her experience as a Black girl facing racism in a majority-white school. She could give several unconnected examples of the slurs slung at her, a teacher's clueless assumptions about her, and the absence of Black characters in the books assigned in class. Her essay could go on to tell how she decided not to become a victim of racism but to fight against it, by forming an anti-racism organization and getting elected its president.

Very impressive. What school wouldn't want her? But a hero's journey approach would turn her account—which, frankly, is little more than a résumé in essay form—into a gripping story. Instead of listing examples of racism, she could describe walking to the bus stop on a beautiful morning, ready to begin her first day in a new school. Her family has just moved to this neighborhood, and her parents have heard great things about the district. She's nervous but excited, eager to learn, and wondering whether she should try out for the volleyball team. Spotting a clump of white kids talking and laughing at the bus stop, she feels a little shy but bravely walks up, smiling. The kids grow silent and stare at her. One of them makes an unflattering comment about her hair. (*Tie*) She sits alone on the bus and tells herself that at least this way she can read her book in peace. (*Untie*) But she had hoped to meet someone who could help her find her way through the school. (*Tie*) Instead she walks in alone, ignoring the stares of the other students. She stops and looks around, wondering where she's supposed to be, when a tall, good-looking boy approaches. "Hey," he says, smiling.

"Hey," she says, feeling her heart race. (*Untie*)

"Want to see something?" He lifts his iPhone to her face. It shows a horrible, racist video. The picture gets blurry through her tears, and she pushes past him and runs down the crowded hallway. (*Tie*)

In her story, this event forces her into another world—not the new neighborhood or school but the world where people can be so cruel to someone who looks like her. At this point she gets the first hint of who she really is: She finds that a small part of her isn't crushed but angry. Gradually, as she faces one trial after another, she begins to talk back, fight, and organize. (*Untie*) At the end—say, her junior year—she faces down the boy who showed her the video. And she realizes that he is the weaker one. She's the hero.

If the student puts in the kind of effort an essay demands—including many painful drafts—she will have more than an advantage over other college applicants. That personal essay can help her discover herself. By telling how she untied the knots in some of life's episodes, she describes the actions that reveal her soul.

(I shouldn't have to add that an essay with that level of tying/untying detail would stump your average AI bot.)

> Exercise: It seems a shame that the college admissions essay gets limited to high schoolers. What if employers asked job candidates to submit a storytelling version of the standard cover letter? Even better, if everyone wrote one before beginning a search for work, that process of soul discovery might make them rethink their careers, choosing one that's more appropriate for their true souls. Imagine a teenaged Barbra Streisand doing that. *I'm applying to be a singer in this club, but my essay shows I'm also an actress!*

You on the Big Screen

But who reads essays anymore, other than bored college admissions officers? There may be an even better way to tell your story: Think of it as a major motion picture. While you may not want to submit a hundred-page screenplay to a studio, a cinematic approach can make you a better storyteller. In turn, that story can bring out your soul in a truly compelling fashion. Just think of your tale in terms of certain **beats**; that's what movie people call Aristotle's episodes.

Every screenplay consists of a series of beats in a particular order. A screenwriter named Blake Snyder made a study of these beats in Hollywood movies, and he came up with a beat-centric system called *Save the Cat*. Snyder concluded that every successful picture contains fifteen beats—an opening image, followed by "theme stated," "setup," "catalyst," and so on.

Unless you plan to write a screenplay (super fun!), you can

focus on just five. *Save the Cat* aficionados call them foundation beats. When you read each one, think about your own desired change.

Catalyst: an inciting incident or life-changing event that catapults the hero into a different world or a new way of thinking. This is an "action" beat, a dramatic scene so impactful that it prevents the hero from returning to her status quo world. In your own life, this could be an accident, a piece of bad news, or a dawning awareness that something is making you increasingly unhappy—a catalyst of some sort.

A woman drives to work on a Friday morning. She has been making this commute for years, listening to the same radio station with the same disc jockeys, and as she sits in traffic, she remembers that she once loved to drive. She recalls a road trip out West that she took with a girlfriend. She insisted on driving, and one unforgettable evening she drove into the sunset, with the empty highway leading to a mountain range. It was like a movie; and, though she doesn't yet realize it, a clue to her soul.

But that was a long time ago. Arriving at work, she gets called into a meeting room with her supervisor, along with the manager of human resources, which the company has creepily renamed "people support." They tell her that her job is being "downsized through a position elimination." Fired, in other words. Her whole life—the routine, the income—all get snatched from under her. She gathers her cubicle items in a humiliating box and does the unemployed walk of shame to the elevator, determined not to cry.

Break into Two: Aristotle wrote that every play consists of three acts. Screenwriters follow this rule for movies. Act 1 has set up the before world, and the Catalyst has shoved the hero out of that world. The next foundation beat begins the second act by having our hero accept the call to action. After much crying and massive ice cream consumption, she scrolls through old pictures of her highway adventures and determines to try something new. This action beat separates the status quo world of act 1 from the new, upside-down world of act 2. On her way to the grocery store, our hero listens to a golden-oldie song, "Convoy," about truckers who drive from Los Angeles all the way to New Jersey without stopping. The song was a big hit during the seventies, and it became a movie that she had streamed once. It was silly, and she loved it. Well. What's stopping her from becoming a trucker? All the way home, she debates the idea. She has no clue how to get a trucker's license, or what it would be like to live life on the road. But she decides to look up truck driving schools when she gets home.

Think of the beginning of a second act in your own life. It doesn't require some impulsive response to your catalyst. Instead, you simply accept that it's time for a change.

Midpoint: the middle of the story, obviously. This usually entails a false victory.

After moving into a hotel in a town with a truck driving school, she earns her class A commercial driver's license with a top exam score. She types up a résumé and submits it to trucking companies, and a couple weeks later she begins her new life as a genuine employed truck driver. Success!

When we watch this part of a movie, we know that there's a lot of screen time left. Clearly, this isn't the end of the story. Something has to go wrong. In my own hyperbolic attempt to run my age up Mount Moosilauke, the Midpoint beat prepared me for the inevitable setbacks. They weren't failures but just part of the "movie." Every good story requires its ups and downs.

All Is Lost: In *Save the Cat* storytelling, the biggest downer comes soon after the Midpoint, when the world seems to collapse on the hero. Blake Snyder even suggested that this beat come with a "whiff of death": a hint of mortality or an actual demise.

Our hero hits the road in a tractor trailer, heading west into the sunset, country music playing on the stereo, and the CB crackling witticisms from other truckers. Her dream has come true! She had expected sexism and cruelty in this traditionally male-dominated field. But it turns out that lots of women drive semis. And while one or two men have hit on her, they were relatively shy and polite. She had a worse time with men in her office job.

Suddenly an antelope darts into her lane. She swerves to avoid it, only to hit a second animal. The truck jackknifes into a ditch. Next thing she knows, she is lying on her side and staring out of a cracked windshield. All is lost. She has killed an innocent creature and wrecked her first truck—her employer's truck.

Break into Three: Here we get the solution to the story, the ultimate untying of the hero's knot. I found this beat to be a great source of hope. It may take a long time to get to act 3 in your personal major motion picture, but it will come. The knot will untie.

The woman discovers that her radio still works, and she calls for help. She squirms through her window and finds that the poor antelope is lying right in the middle of the highway. The evening light is dimming. She climbs back into the cab and grabs a box of flares, limps back up onto the road—she realizes her hip has a bad bruise—and ignites the flares. Then she drags the carcass off to the side of the road.

State police show up a couple minutes later, along with an ambulance. The cops praise her for her quick action. The truck eventually gets towed, and her employer reports that the damage isn't serious. The supervisor asks if she needs some time off, and she surprises herself by asking to get right back onto the road. Over the CB, a trucker gives her a new handle: Loper. Hunter of antelopes. She smiles and rides off into another sunset.

Okay, not a great movie. And professional screenwriters tell me that few of them use the *Save the Cat* system. (On the other hand, I find myself spotting the beats in every movie I watch, so there must be something to it.) Assuming your Hyperbole won't involve a movie blockbuster, when you tell yourself your story beat by beat, you can bring out your own heroic soul by tying the action to your deepest needs. Our fictional trucker finds hers through her need for highway adventure, along with her responses to each tangled beat. In the end, she aligns her daily self with her noble soul.

To help make the story more believable—and allow you to believe in your own heroism—consider adding some narrative spices; I call them dramatic goodies. For instance, every great story shows the character's flaws. Nobody's perfect, but the imperfections can make a hero seem more likeable. And correcting a flaw can be part of the heroic journey. (Blake Snyder called this Six Things That Need Fixing.) It's interesting to think of fixable items—circumstances, habits, environment—that actions or luck might resolve or untangle. The list itself reveals something about the fixable soul.

Save the Cat is another Snyder tool, which explains the name of the system. Even the most unlikeable, grumpy, manly-man hero needs to show a soft side. Have him save a cat, or wince when the nurse treats his wound. At times when you most regret saying something cruel, or passing by someone in pain, it helps to think of your own cat-saving moment. How would your life's movie soften your character?

To increase the drama in my mountain Hyperbole, I gave myself a deadline. I would attempt to run my age on my birthday, regardless of the weather or conditions on the mountain that day. Deadlines are stressful, but if you convert them into a kind of literary tension, they can make you root for the character. Could I complete all the training in time? Deadlines are horrible; dramatized deadlines are exciting. To defuse the bomb before the bus blows up . . . horrible, but compelling. You're not completing a project; you're defusing a bomb! This is all about kairos—suiting the timing to the narrative chaos. Deadlines can seem debilitating, but I find it helpful to see them as dramatic devices in my own daily life.

Lastly, every movie needs a poster with a good motto. "Love means never having to say you're sorry." "Man is the warmest place to hide." "The first casualty of war is innocence." In my own self-story, a doctor told me, "Pain is a signal." It became a motto. Your own motto need not be witty or profound. Don't shrink from a sappy cliché. "Music is the purest connection." "A language shouldn't be foreign." "Exercise is just purer breathing." Repeat it enough in your head and it can seem just right.

This kind of storytelling, with its foundation beats and tools, does not conflict with the hero's journey. Both yank a character out of a before world and put her into an upside-down environment, where she faces challenges, confronts a moment of truth, and ends up with a well-earned bit of wisdom. Even if your only desire at the moment is to lose some weight or find the courage to change jobs, it helps to put your goal into a story.

> Exercise: Instead of making it all about your past, tell a story about your own future. Craft it as if you're writing a treatment to submit to a movie studio. Cast yourself as the hero who triumphs in the end and—crucially—finds her true soul.

If you struggle to come up with a good story about your future heroic self, don't despair. Your story just might come out of your Hyperbole.

THE TOOLS

<u>Event connections</u>. Aristotle teaches that a good tale convinces the audience that everything happening to a character results from a previous event. She spends the story untying every problem, only to face another, right up until the end of the plot. This tool can help us with our own stories. We often feel stymied by the cascade of problems in our lives. We solve one, only to face another. By creating a narrative of our lives that extends into the future—connecting the real previous events with fictional future ones—we can gain some belief that our lives won't always be filled with knots.

<u>Hero's journey</u>. This classic plot has the main character—you—leave the realm of normality, pushed into a quest by a crisis or the awareness of a deep need. You face the monsters or bad guys, acquire allies, and triumph in the end. Most important, you gain some wisdom about life, or about yourself.

<u>Beats</u>. In telling your past or future story, follow the *Save the Cat* foundational beats: Catalyst, Break into Two, Midpoint, All Is Lost, Break into Three. Aristotle would likely approve. Every great story comprises three acts, he said. (He was talking about plays, thousands of years before the invention of the novel, but plot is plot. Great

stories have three acts.) By turning your tale into a virtual movie, you become your very own hero.

Dramatic goodies. Six Things That Need Fixing might provide a way to assay your soul. Why exactly do they need fixing? And how can you tell a tale where at least some of them get fixed? Soften your self-story with an adorable Save the Cat quirk. Consider a scary defuse-the-bomb deadline for motivation and extra excitement. Then give your imaginary movie poster a slogan. ("A new job is a mission.")

12

Experimentation

Test the Tools

An exemplarily stupid and pointless feat

"And if one thing is possible, then so is the other; and if the harder of a pair is possible, then so is the easier."

—Aristotle, *Rhetoric*

At six o'clock in the morning of my fifty-eighth birthday, I am about to put the rhetorical tools to the ultimate test.

I stand shivering at the base of a weather-torn slickrock mountain in New Hampshire wearing nothing but running shorts and "minimalist" shoes that are more slippers than shoes. Beside me blasts the Baker River, named after a Colonial-era soldier who warred against the local Abenaki Indians.

I have pictured this moment countless times, creating the anticipatory story of a triumph of self-persuasion. The idea of running my age up Moosilauke, reaching the top in less than fifty-eight minutes, constitutes my personal Hyperbole, an attempt to throw myself beyond the reasonable. The simple act of running already counts as an achievement; just a year ago, I struggled to walk without a limp.

My rapidly aging body offers an experiment in kairos. I will find an opening through the chaos of pain and desire. What's more, my birthday qualifies as a synecdoche: a single day representing all the years of my life. This is why I'm attempting this feat on my birthday. By turning fifty-eight in official years, I give myself a whole other minute to run my age.

Besides, my birthday offers a sort of movie-beat countdown: The clock is ticking. I have just one chance. To raise the stakes, I have gathered some four thousand followers on a Facebook page titled Breaking the Time Barrier. These followers, along with my friends, inject an element of fear—a test, Aristotle would say, of my own perceived skill and agency. My confidence will come from my development of my ethos, the pairing of my daily self with my noble Aristotelian soul.

Right up to this moment, my year-long personal experiment in self-persuasion has mostly seemed like a good idea. My use of the Tortoise Method and Aristotle's Lure & Ramp has allowed me to carve out training time and build the eating and workout habits I needed. At four o'clock this morning, I stood on our bathroom scale and found that I had shed a sixth of my body weight. Every pound I have lost is a pound I no longer have to hoist up this mountain. "I can practically grate cheese on my abs," I informed Dorothy, who tactfully avoided rolling her eyes.

Years from now, I will look at a photo a friend took on that day. It reveals more cadaver than X-Man. Dorothy was calling me her whippet. But today, on my hyperbolic age-run day, I am in my own mind a perfectly tuned athletic machine.

I wipe the mist off the face of my running watch and stare at the zeros. Only a dozen people have ever run their age up this classic peak, and none was over fifty. On the other hand, few fellow geezers have been foolish enough to try. The winds above the tree line can blow hard enough to pick up a skinny guy like me and toss him like a leaf. The Abenaki had the good sense to avoid the summit, believing that an angry god squatted up there.

My wife stands behind me at the start line, here to cheer me on along with our friends Robert, Jes, and Lydia, all hugging themselves in the cool August mist. This morning Dorothy got up before me and taped my training charms all over the house, including the paeans *My legs love rocks, I flow up rocks,* and *I'm strong and light and taking flight.*

It had taken a lot to get here. The training really started with medically induced pain. When I told my doctor about my Hyperbole, rather than calling me an idiot, she gave me the name of a sports medicine specialist in Vermont. "He runs and skis," she said. "He'll get you." The doctor was experimenting with a procedure called neural prolotherapy. Invented in New Zealand, it entailed multiple injections of dextrose into the nerves. "Your gluteal muscles are weak because they're constantly firing from the pain," he explained.

And then he proceeded to give me 180 shots in one session.

While sweating through the stings, I thought about how painful running up Moosilauke would be, and I called on my rhetoric. *This isn't therapy,* I told myself, reframing the torture. *It's training.* And somehow the idea—that I wasn't just recovering but hyperbolically throwing myself way beyond—made the pain not just tolerable but sort of cool. The shots were training me to suffer, turning the agony into a test of character. To be honest, this was not easy. Each shot felt like the sting of a wasp, and after a couple dozen of them I was ready to tell the doctor anything to make him stop. I returned for more shots weekly, needing fewer injections each time as the pain diminished. I supplemented the shots with at least an hour a day of resistance training, foam rolling, and stretching. After a few months, my hips stopped snapping. I walked with a subtle limp.

I began waking at four in the morning, and eventually took to running up the meadow behind our house. I ramped up to three hours of training per day, gradually adding resistance and cardio workouts until they felt like a normal job. My weeks consisted of two days of high-intensity intervals; one long, slow endurance run; two medium runs; a recovery day of stretching; and a rest day, plus three or four easy runs throughout the week.

In order to carry minimal weight on my five-foot-eleven frame, I gave up drinking and cut out just about every enjoyable food. I dropped to a ribs-baring 144 pounds. My wife suffered at least as much as I did. Embracing me must have felt like hugging a birch tree. Friends asked her delicate questions about my health, even while I flexed shirtless and bored her with explanations of the distinction between anabolism and catabolism. Yet (I married a saint) she feigned interest in the whole thing.

Now, on my birthday, she and my friends stand behind me at the Moosilauke start line. The trail ahead rears up from the Baker River like a shying horse. It's all ascent from here; or, as trail runners like to say, this run has only one hill. I draw a deep breath, trying to look confident, and start my watch. I hear sleepy cheers as I mince down a jumble of rocks and across a slippery bridge that spans the Baker. I take rapid little steps with high-pistoning knees, struggling to increase my rhythm to the ideal 180 beats per minute. The Gorge Brook pounds past me.

Forcing myself to smile even while gasping for air, I whisper a one-word charm for this first stretch:

Relax.

I've always been an evidence-based, show-me skeptic, one of little faith. You won't catch me willingly trying anything with *alternative* in front of it. I resisted using charms at first but had run out of reasonable options; rhetoric was the only one left. Besides, every coach and athlete I spoke to insisted that charms work. So every day, when my alarm went off at four A.M., I said aloud my wakeup paean, "Make this a glorious day." I began the day with breathing exercises, repeating ridiculous, paean-adjacent expressions:

> *Running is my natural state.*
> *My legs love rocks. I flow up rocks.*
> *I'm strong and light and taking flight.*

Gradually, the expressions stopped sounding trite and began to seem true. By golly, I *was* strong and light and about to take flight!

I extended my use of charms and divided the mountain into four rhetorically friendly sections: relax, flow, focus, and dance. Once a week for several months I arrived at the Moosilauke trailhead before dawn to run in first light, pausing to rest between sections. Athletes call this interval training; in rhetoric, it's chunking: turning the mountain into a literal ramp and reframing each chunk.

I force a smile to help myself relax. I'm a bona fide athlete. I'm having fun, and running up steep, slippery rocks hardly hurts at all!

It hurts a lot. *Smile.*

Because snow had lingered on the mountain well into May, my training was limited to this first chunk until June. Then the snow turned into mud so deep that, more than once, I had to crawl out of gooey sinkholes, more mud wrestler than trail runner. Today this section feels, well, somewhat less wet. I tell myself to *relax*, right up until the brook vanishes into a spring known as Last Water, where hikers can still reliably fill their water bottles before continuing their ascent. I enter the next section.

Flow.

The trail flattens out a bit after Last Water, letting me pick up speed and run with what ease I can muster. The state of flow is fleeting, requiring a constant effort to achieve effortlessness. Nature, like life, does everything to throw you off your stride and break your rhythm. Frequent travel, injuries, and illness all sought to interrupt my training. Torrential rains have washed away a section of trail and forced a reroute that lengthens my run. This is nature's version of an aging event, adding thirty seconds or more—the equivalent of half a year—to my total.

I don't try to psych myself up for the change. Instead, I resort to choicelessness—the force of habit, keeping my flow all the way to a spot on the trail called First View. Here, at three thousand feet of elevation, Dartmouth student volunteers have chopped down trees to open up the vista, and on a clear day, the vast Presidential Range is visible to the northeast. But today I don't look at anything but the trail. I blast through First View, force myself not to peek at my watch, and head toward the steepest part of the trail.

Focus.

Exercise-induced asthma kicks in as I navigate the mixture of scree and car-sized boulders. I croak with every exhalation. My legs feel as if they're rusting in the morning mist, and my eyes film over, blurring my vision—a side effect of low blood sugar. Over the years, I've had mild hallucinations on this stretch of trail, spotting nonexistent people, glimpsing spectral moose, hearing ravens utter human sounds. The angry god atop Moosilauke may be having his way with me.

Why am I doing this? Why can't I be a normal person and enjoy my approaching golden years instead of trying to prove something that no one but me cares about?

Focus.

I dash up a second steep stretch, then a third, where the trail turns left and the rising sun hits my back. The temperature at the trailhead had been an alarming sixty-two, more than twenty degrees warmer than ideal, with 80 percent humidity. And now the brutal, unbridled rays of heat. Even in my prime years I dreaded this turn. I would slow to a walk or stop altogether, bent over and gasping. I used to think of this place as "where I get hot and fall to pieces." Now I've reframed it as Bright Corner. The label goes with all the redefining I've done on this mountain. The hard parts are now "fun parts," the steep ledges are mere "rocks," and the pain, "suffering." This welcoming of the overwhelming is not pain at all. It's life with all the stops open. I came to realize that suffering, rhetorically understood, is a kind of motivation.

The trail rises up a series of steps—rocks levered into place long ago by strong young volunteers—and then narrows to less than a foot wide in some stretches, with a spectacular view toward the northwest. I studiously ignore it. Another set of steps leads to a promontory where I use my hands and feet to ascend. I top out to my first look at the summit, across a barren, lonesome ridge.

The path dips into a col filled with stunted spruce and sharp rocks that perverse geology has tilted on their sides like upended radial saws. They rip the thin fabric of my shoes and bruise the soles of my feet, and still I must sprint as fast as I can here to gain time.

Dance.

Instead of feeling frustrated by the paradox of prancing through radial saws, I've convinced myself to think of this stretch as pure dancing—not pretty dancing, but dancing nonetheless.

I emerge from the stunted trees onto the ridge. Thankfully, no wind today. A tiny speck of orange appears in the distance: the summit sign. I'm out of gas, with nothing but desire to take me the rest of the way.

Or maybe it's not desire so much as a strange, compelling form of happiness. Recent studies of psychedelic drugs have shown similar states in people given psilocybin, a milder cousin of LSD. Volunteers who took the drug reported feeling at one with the universe, emitting John Lennon–esque utterances like "Love is all!" I felt like this once before, while climbing Mount Rainier to celebrate my fortieth birthday. I was with a group of capable, friendly men, two of them former guides on the mountain, and we took a more technical route than the usual climb. As the least experienced of the bunch, I was scared the whole time. The effort of climbing on a glacier above fourteen thousand feet while shouldering a heavy pack felt like running back-to-back marathons. Yet, the higher we got, the happier I became. I could feel my ego dropping away, as if I became less important and somehow joined the beautiful, white-blue landscape, my dear friends, and . . . something even larger and holier. Seriously, I felt at one with the universe. And now, as I float along the ridge on Moosilauke, I feel the same way.

I think of Dorothy waking up extra early to tape my charms all over the house, and of the four thousand friends on Facebook wishing me luck. One close friend wrote, "My hand will be on your back." I have to focus just to keep my eyes from tearing up.

One last scramble up a small pinnacle, and I slap the sign at the top and punch my watch. There's little chance of a time of less than fifty-eight minutes—the day is too warm, and I feel too good to have given the effort needed. But, goal or no goal, I'm happier than I've felt in many years. I savor the moment, gazing out toward the soaring Presidential Peaks before checking my watch for the first time since the start.

54:53

I blink hard, my vision still cloudy.

54:53

I stare at this representation of my age in minutes, which means I have set back my personal clock more than three years. And for a brief moment I consider: If conditions had been ideal—if the trail had been dry, the day cooler, the air less humid—could I have run myself right back into my forties? It's possible. Yet the thought does not give me any more joy. I couldn't possibly feel more joy. All my attempts at self-manipulation, all the Aristotelian soul bending tools I had used to turn myself into an athlete . . . they actually worked. But I hadn't expected this feeling.

Researchers who conduct psychedelic therapy say that the one-with-the-universe, love-is-all effects tend to last at least a year. (I'm writing this ten years after that moment on the summit and can still feel the connection and the love.) On this summit, at this moment of my glorious birthday, I look up from my watch and don't feel like yelling or raising my arms in triumph. Instead I whisper, *Thank you.*

The angry god is silent.

Part 4

SOLUTION

13

Joy

Find Happiness

Why the lama giggled

"Happiness does not lie in amusement; it would be strange if one were to take trouble and suffer hardship all one's life in order to amuse oneself."

—Aristotle, *Nicomachean Ethics*

When I was a student at a small college, back in the mid-seventies, the religion department invited me to have breakfast with a Tibetan monk. I was editor of the student newspaper, and the department chair presumably hoped that the invitation would lead to an article. Preferring to sleep in, I asked my news editor, Stan, to take my place. "It's tomorrow at eight," I told him. "You get up early anyway."

Stan looked up from his typewriter. (Yes, it was that long ago. But it was an *electric* typewriter.) "Who did you say it was?"

"His name is Dolly something." I looked down at the invitation.

"It says he's a lama, with one *l*." And for a moment I thought this might be some kind of joke.

"The *Dalai Lama*?" Stan, who was much more cued into the universe than I—he went on to become a leading geneticist—grabbed the invitation from my hand. He read it and nodded. "You have to go. He's, like, the leader of a whole branch of Buddhism. The holiest of holy men. I think the Tibetans even consider him some kind of god." So I went, mostly to see what a god eats for breakfast.

In my defense, the Dalai Lama was not quite the international celebrity he is today. (And Google did not exist back then, obviously.) At age twenty-four, the monk had fled Tibet in fear for his life after calling for independence from the Chinese government. When I met him, he was forty years old, head of state of the Tibetan government in exile, and on a tour of the United States. I showed up late in a dining hall. The Dalai Lama was sitting at a table with the religion professor and an interpreter. He wore drapey red robes and aviator glasses. He had a crew cut. I can't recall what I asked him, or what we talked about. All I remember is that the man giggled the entire time. I was unimpressed. After breakfast, I banged out a paragraph on the Buddhist monk who visited campus and forgot about the whole thing.

About a decade later, I was working in Washington, D.C., and someone in the office mentioned that the Dalai Lama was coming to America. I said, "The guy from Tibet? I had breakfast with him."

Dead silence. It was as if I had name-dropped the Buddha himself, which made it all the more embarrassing that I could recall almost nothing about the encounter. He was just this giggling little man who seemed to have nothing memorable to say.

In the years since, though, I've thought a lot about why the man laughed so much. Maybe he was amused by a clueless student editor. But it was probably more than that. Buddhist friends tell me that some monks do laugh a lot.

The Dalai Lama had had every reason *not* to laugh. He had lost his homeland. The CIA had had to help extract him from Tibet. He was the spiritual leader of millions, and the head of a government. Yet here he was, sitting at a table in a small college's dining hall, laughing. I've since come to realize that his laughter may be some kind of achievement.

If this seems a bit of a non sequitur in a book about ancient Greeks and self-persuasion, consider: Modern scholarship has discovered that South Asia and Greece were talking to each other in ancient times. Today we can see some striking parallels between Buddhism—established around the sixth century BCE—and Greek philosophy that developed soon after. While there's no evidence that the Greeks were directly influenced by the Buddhists, we do know that trade between Greece and India had been flourishing for centuries. In fact, the Greeks coined the word *India*. (The Indians in turn called the Greeks "Yonas," the people of Ionia.) Some of the oldest Greek myths had gods and heroes—Dionysius and Herakles among others—who practically commuted between the two regions. We can easily imagine wanderlustful Sophists serving as ambassadors on trading missions and picking up some Buddhist philosophy along the way.

It's no accident that the Sophists' approach to happiness might sound similar to that of the Dalai Lama. Both sought happiness as a goal. This chapter will cover the techniques that the Greeks came up with—methods that just may have you someday achieve the art of laughing at breakfast.

First let's clarify what we mean by *happiness*. The word entered the English language from the old Scandinavian word *happ*. It had two definitions, according to the *OED*. *Happ* meant good fortune, a positive happenstance. It also meant "the state of pleasurable contentment of the mind." Happiness comes from luck, yes, but also from our interpretation of that fortune. It's a gift from the gods, along with—here's where the interpretation comes in—a strong dose of self-persuasion.

Now, it just so happens that *happiness* (the word, not the mood) reached the British Isles just when the Viking raiders were pillaging the coast. You can imagine these cheerful thugs drinking and singing by the fire after a good raid, clapping along because they felt like a room without a roof. No wonder those singing Vikings seemed happy. One imagines the locals grasping only the luck part of the definition; the contentment aspect might have come later. Language works in mysterious ways, its wonders to perform.

Two thousand years before the Vikings arrived in Britannia, Aristotle had added a third quality to happiness: a person's own management of his circumstances. Genuine long-term happiness requires a set of actions that align your daily self with your soul. Not that Aristotle would have disagreed with the Vikings. He wrote that luck and interpretation also contribute.

So, in Aristotle's philosophy, happiness comes from a trifecta: fortune, functioning, and framing. The happiest people have inherited good luck. They live virtuous lives. And they frame their circumstances in a positive light.

Fortune: The Thread Cutter

To understand Aristotle's attitude toward fate, and how rhetoric can deal with life's slings, arrows, and lottery winnings, we have to go even further back in time. The early Greeks had gods for luck; these were the Fates. The first Fate, Clotho (the spinner), spun the thread of life. Next came Lachesis (the allotter), who measured the length of the thread. Then the third Fate—Atropos (the *a* means "not" or "never," and *tropos,* remember, means "turning")—Atropos, the unbending, the One Who Could Not Be Turned, cut the thread. Every inch of that thread contained the story of a person's life. (Interestingly, the Vikings had almost the exact same myth.) Odysseus, the man Homer called polytropos, defied the Fates with his many turnings. So did Aristotle, in his own way. The philosopher refused to believe that our lives are spun in advance.

Well, not entirely. Happiness, Aristotle said, requires a kind of "virtuous welfare"—inherited benefits plus the capacity to procure them. The natural advantages include "gentle birth, a wide circle of friends, a virtuous circle of friends, wealth, creditable offspring, extensive offspring, and a comfortable old age." Happiness also relies on attributes of your body and what you make of them: "health, beauty, strength, size, and competitive prowess." Your reputation and social status help. And, finally, there's your soul and its positive elements: "prudence, courage, justice, and moderation." In Aristotle's world, a popular, rich, hard-bodied nobleman would tend to be happy. (Women, alas, lacked wealth and status, so the Greeks were thinking only of male happiness.)

These days, celebrity counts as nobility. Think of the actors who played in the X-Men movies. The Fates have been kind to them by granting them good-looking ancestors. In other words, you could say that our modern Fates are the genes we inherit from our forebears. Not a morning person? Our genes determined that! Addicted to chocolate? Genes! Genetic fatalism leads us to believe that our IQ, or our native laziness or empathy, comes from our DNA. If Aristotle were around today, he might say that these amino acid threads do spin our lives; but we mortals still have agency. His deliberative rhetoric, argument that leads to choices, depends on a philosophy of contingency. Every situation is an unpredictable moment, and we can decide what to do with that moment. Our choices, in return, compete with the Fates in determining our future. Did Lachesis the allotter measure your life with a short thread? Will DNA, the oddsmaker, hit you with a heart attack after fifty? That depends in part on what you do.

Functioning: The Better Angel

The ancient Greeks put special emphasis on the personal management part of the good-life formula—the aspect that links actions with the soul. Their term for happiness was *eudaimonia*. Among the earliest Greeks, a *daimon* was a resident spirit; hence the English word *demon*. Lucky you if your daimon was a good spirit, a *eudaimon*. It would whisper sound advice, setting you on the right path and helping you resist temptation. Socrates claimed to have a eudaimon that steered him away from mistakes. He said this voice in his head was even more accurate than reading entrails.

A *cacodaimon,* on the other hand, was an evil spirit who would lead you into temptation. Some Greeks believed you could have a pair of daimons inside you, constantly debating choices. It's where we get those cartoon images of the devil and angel sitting on a person's shoulders. In some instances—the movie *Animal House* comes to mind—both daimons appear as miniature versions of the character himself. "You know she wants it," the devil version of Pinto tells him. "For shame!" the angel Pinto replies. "If you lay one finger on that poor, sweet, helpless girl, you'll despise yourself forever!"

This dual-angel myth cut no ice with Aristotle. He believed that just one daimon resides in each of us. It's our own soul, one that leans devilish or angelic. We can push back against the Fates,

Odysseus-style, with our own behavior. In other words, the Fates weave our thread—or, in modern terms, deal our hand. Our eudaimonia depends on how we play our cards. With our actions—particularly our daily habits—we can bend our daimon toward the angelic. Our souls motivate us toward our actions; in return, our actions change our souls. Winston Churchill put it metaphorically: "We shape our houses, and then they shape us."

Aristotle converted the Fates into certain odds you can work with: You could deal with your genetic inheritance with McDonald's and Jack Daniel's, or with a daily walk and vegetables. These choices don't always appear as writing on the wall. You lack complete data. You can only weigh choices; and then you have no clear idea how your decisions will affect the future.

Suppose you're a recent high school graduate with good grades, respectable board scores, and an ability to fix things around the house. You could go to college, major in philosophy, and accumulate more debt in graduate school. You could end up in one of many respectable, high-earning careers, or possibly find yourself teaching in a community college for a salary somewhat lower than a manager's pay at an Applebee's. Or you could take your high school degree, skip college, and move to Bellingham, Washington, where the average plumber makes more than a hundred grand a year. You could eventually start your own plumbing business, retire early, and study philosophy. Which is the better choice? That depends. A good argument could be made for either one.

The secret to making these choices is to separate your appetites—your greedy little desires—from your soul's true needs. We saw in chapter one how emphasizing needs over wants, setting up good habits, will align your behavior with your soul and help you accomplish your goals. Aristotle would say that this alignment does not just lead to happiness. It *counts* as happiness.

Whether you recognize this fact depends on the third characteristic of eudaimonia: framing.

Framing: Atomic Happiness

The first self-help philosophies arose from argument that centered around defining the good life. What is the good life to you? A "happy" one? Say that to any politician, or an MBA scrambling up the corporate ladder, or an aspiring actor waiting tables in New York's theater district. We moderns tend to think of the good life in terms of accomplishment, possessions, or recreation. The good life for an ambitious person is success—power, money, fame, or all three. On the other hand, ask a teenager to define the good life, and she might focus on a clear complexion and a killer gaming setup.

The ancients weren't in agreement about the ways to achieve happiness or even how to frame the idea of the good life. One group of Athenians insisted on defining happiness in terms of behavior. The purpose of life was to live well, they said; and by "well" they meant virtuously. Their idea of virtue was not that different from Aristotle's: wisdom, courage, moderation, and justice—standing up for what's right, applying reason to every decision. These philosophers and students gathered in the Stoa Poikile—the Painted Porch, a covered colonnade that fronted one of Athens's largest buildings in the agora. The group called itself the Stoics, and they taught *apatheia*, or apathy: a state of mind free from passions. (These days, there are drugs for that.) The Stoics applied heroic doses of rhetoric that would connect them to the universe—which they believed was an overarching rational soul, or *logos*.

The passions the Stoics most tried to avoid were distress (an awareness of present evil), delight (an awareness of a present good), fear (a feeling of impending danger), and lust (a desire distinct from the soul's true needs, including not just one-night stands but tasty meals). While the Stoics could hardly be called laugh riots, they weren't averse to being happy. In fact, they believed that a truly virtuous person *was* happy. He could be sick, enslaved, or under torture, and so long as he practiced virtue and apathy, his pain and loss—mere passions—would mean nothing to him. He could smile through his agony.

It's just that happiness was not the point. Virtue was. The good life meant being good. The founder of Stoicism, Zeno of Citium, had some, shall we say, original ideas about being good. For instance, he dealt with lust philosophically, by proposing the abolition of marriage. Women would be shared, and boys would be educated in sex by having coitus with girls and with each other. A QAnon nightmare, basically.

Shorn of its weirder aspects, Stoicism flourished in ancient Rome; Cicero occasionally called himself a Stoic, and the emperor Marcus Aurelius wrote his famous *Meditations* to promote the philosophy. Early Christians picked up Stoicism and leaned into the good-life-as-virtue ethic. The Stoics believed that virtue came from behavior connecting their individual souls with the universal logos. The early Christians took up the idea. In their eyes, the purpose of life was to connect the soul to God. The good life was the life that led to the afterlife. Happiness, they hoped, would come later.

One group of Athenian philosophers did see happiness as the whole point of a good life. They met in a garden owned by a man named Epicurus of Samos. While the Stoics sought apathy, Epicurus taught *ataraxia*, freedom from disturbance. The Stoics believed in ignoring pain; the Epicureans sought to avoid it altogether. The Stoically minded Christians later libeled the Epicureans with a reputation for drunken feasts, but the philosophers in Epicurus's Garden served meals that would hardly show up in any restaurant today. They ate a vegetarian gruel, and Epicurus wrote that a piece of cheese would qualify as a feast. Instead of the rumored wild orgies, they entertained themselves with philosophical conversation. Happiness, for these people, depended on avoiding the kinds of behavior that would lead to regrets later.

But only during their lifetime. An Epicurean's future was limited to the length of his or her mortal life. (Unlike all the other philosophical schools, the Garden welcomed women.) The soul dies with the body, thanks to some modern-sounding physics. Epicurus argued that everything, including the soul, is made up of atoms (from the Greek *atomos*, meaning "indivisible"), tiny particles whose movements drive our fates. When we die, those atoms disperse and join the rest of the universe. Meanwhile, atoms occasionally "swerve," creating gaps in the fabric of fate and offering us humans opportunities to practice free will. The concept isn't unlike mutations in biology—genetic "swerves" that allow species to adapt to a changing environment.

The Fourfold Cure-All

While the Stoics focused on staying virtuous and bearing life's pains and misfortunes stoically, the Epicureans took their happiness-focused philosophy one step further. Rather than just pursuing happiness, they came up with a cure for *unhappiness*. Being skilled rhetoricians, they based their remedy on a metaphor. A popular drug in ancient Greece, the *tetrapharmakos,* combined four popular remedies into a single super-cure; think NyQuil, only with herbs. The rhetorical tetrapharmakos of the Epicureans cured four mental diseases: fear of god's punishment, fear of death, fear of pain, and anxiety about earthly goods.

What does any of this have to do with you and me? Assume for the sake of this chapter that we equate a good life with a happy one. Would a meal plan of oatmeal and cheese really make us happy? Could we cheerfully swap quiet conversation for Netflix? And why would we be interested in the tetrapharmakos when we have actual pharmacies, stocked not with metaphors but with actual, physical drugs?

I don't mean these to be rhetorical questions; not entirely. But on first encountering the Epicureans' tetrapharmakos, I couldn't help thinking of the breakfasting Dalai Lama. He seemed to be free of the four angsty "diseases" that Epicurus listed.

Fear of God's punishment: As a Buddhist, the lama does not share the Judeo-Christian view of an angry God. Nor did the Epicureans. While they believed in the gods, they thought that these self-absorbed divine beings did not deign to bother themselves with human affairs. Why would the mighty gods—themselves made up of atoms but blessed with superpowers and immortality—get miffed at some tiny mortal's peccadillos? That notion was just egotistical on humans' part. As a result, the Epicureans did not go in for the concept of guilt. They saw it as a negative "passion" that would block ataraxia.

Fear of death: Buddhists and Epicureans both share the belief that death is a transition rather than a horror. Their doctrines split off from there; while Buddhists hold that we transit from one life to another, the Epicureans believed that our atoms simply join the rest of the universe.

Western societies could use this fourfold rhetorical medicine. Many of us measure a life by length rather than quality. We consider a short life filled with rich adventure and noble acts to be a tragedy that ends too soon. A long, boring, meaningless life is a kind of success, because—congratulations! You lived to a hundred! We tend to frame the end of life as a battle against disease, a fight we inevitably lose.

Both the Stoics and Epicureans agreed with Aristotle in teaching that death is not painful. Life is. Epicurus wrote that, as long as you and I exist, death does not. And once we die, we no longer exist, so death literally has nothing to do with us. This idea led to inscriptions you can still see on ancient Roman gravestones: *Non fui, fui, non sum, non curo.* I was not; I was; I am not; I do not care. A philosophical approach to fear of death treats it as a fallacy. If you don't exist, how can you fear nonexistence?

Fear of pain. This one may be the toughest for us to cure. That's because we tend to see pain itself as a disease. The doctors who are most conservative about prescribing pain meds get the lowest ratings from their patients. We've developed a zero-tolerance attitude toward pain, and this has led to an unprecedented outbreak of addiction. No rational person would describe your average addict as happy.

Not to say that someone in chronic pain should avoid doctors. But the Epicureans understood that the fearful anticipation of pain often makes us avoid pursuing most of the goals we've covered in this book—particularly those requiring exercising, risk-taking, and self-denial. We've already seen the prophylactic remedy: the rhetorical trick of framing pain as suffering. While the ancients realized that this takes practice, true mastery of pain can actually relieve pain.

Anxiety about earthly goods. If your needs are modest, you have fewer worries about meeting them. I can't imagine the Dalai Lama complaining about the quality of food in our college dining hall. And while the Epicurean diet would not make any American's mouth water, it was easy to provide. If you cared to follow that menu—oatmeal for breakfast and lunch, cheese and boxed wine from Target for dinner—you would spend less than three dollars a day.

Epicurus provided a taxonomy of desires. *Natural and necessary* desires include minimal food and shelter. *Natural and unnecessary* desires comprise sex and dessert. Then there are the *vain and empty* desires: a thousand Instagram followers, a brooch from Tiffany's.

Aristotle would agree with these definitions. Distinguishing between our appetites and the soul's true needs would lead to a simple life. The truly good things, those that satisfy our true needs, are the easiest to obtain. Our unnecessary appetites lead to regret and pain. The quest to satisfy those appetites leads to anxiety about money. And anxiety is a disease.

But there's no need to be an extreme Epicurean. The philosophy itself preaches moderation and offers an ancient notion of freedom.

Wonder of Wonders

All this talk might make you feel that happiness is limited to something you accumulate with skill, like a well-chosen stock portfolio. It's true that a happy life is not a temporary thing. Aristotle would argue that good habits are more powerful over the long term than today's more fashionable disciplines—mindfulness, gratitude, and the like. But Aristotle also believed that eudaimonia can lead to those other things. The Greeks had a word for the kind of sublime wonder we experience in numinous moments: *thaumaston*.

Years ago, one of the first viral memes featured Double Rainbow Guy, a man who posted a video of a rainbow while enthusing over the view: "It's a freakin' double rainbow! Oh, gosh, I can't believe it!" Comedians made fun of his over-the-top joy. "This is so intense!" Double Rainbow Guy gushes, crying. But that gushing guy was arguably primed for the experience. He had not rushed off, head down, to work. He was standing in a field, looking up, experiencing thaumaston: a sublime instant. A certain level of Aristotelian happiness can allow you Double Rainbow moments—not just the scenes themselves but a complete surrender to them.

The Roman poet Lucretius, who wrote *The Nature of Things*, an epic poem dedicated to Epicureanism, described just that kind of state:

> *Such revelations and I'm seized by a divine delight—*
> *I shiver, for, due to your power, Nature everywhere*
> *In every part lies open; all her secrets are laid bare.*

By "your power" he meant Epicurus's philosophy of disciplined happiness. In joining the daily self to the soul, Lucretius believed, you attach yourself to the atom-rich universe.

I believe a capital-*H* Hyperbole can help push that pursuit. Mountain peaks aid with that, literally as well as metaphorically. In the alpine zone, the great climber Willi Unsoeld said, you may reach the purest zone of all. Psychologists call it egolessness. Buddhists call it Ananda. Christians call it the peace that passes all understanding.

Assuming you're not an alpine climber, could you reach that zone with a different, more virtual kind of peak?

I believe, yes.

THE TOOLS

The tetrapharmakos. This fourfold rhetorical medicine offers freedom from four chronic fears:

Fear of divine punishment. Regardless of your religious belief, the Epicureans held that life's daily accidents—the opportunities opened up by those swerving atoms—make us responsible for our own happiness. By living moderately and virtuously, we can connect our daily selves to our Aristotelian souls, which in turn joins us to the universal soul. Or to God, if you like.

Fear of death. First there was no you. Then there was you. Then there won't be you, in which case you won't care. This cure doesn't have to conflict with Judeo-Christian doctrine. Some believers interpret heaven as a kind of great joining.

Fear of pain. Reframing pain as an ability to suffer helps you to withstand the pain, and to commit to the discomfort of achieving change.

Anxiety about earthly goods. Aristotle provided the cure for income anxiety before Epicurus was born. Learn to distinguish between your appetites and your soul's true needs, and you will spend less. Wealth is a feeling, not a metric.

Thaumaston. A state of surprise and wonder in sublime moments. This tool depends on an ability to be open to double rainbows, and an awareness of their importance. It helps to have a soul that's sufficiently well aligned to avoid the public embarrassment of displaying your awe.

14

Peroration

Tap the Power of Words

The why of being human

"It may be said that every individual man and all men in common aim at a certain end which determines what they choose and what they avoid. This end . . . is happiness and its constituents."

—Aristotle, *Rhetoric*

Many years ago, at a time when the classics had already become unfashionable, a professor at Dartmouth College scheduled a course in ancient Greek. Only one student signed up. The professor went ahead and taught the class. A colleague considered this a terrible use of the man's time. "Why are you teaching a whole class for one person?"

The Greek scholar bellowed, "To save his immortal soul!"

Whether or not I succeeded in running my age, a reasonable person might consider the attempt a waste of time. Why would I put so much effort into something that would never earn me a prize while demanding lung-burning intensity, torturous endurance, and bad weather? And why should you attempt something equally horrible? The old professor would doubtless say it's to save our souls.

To be perfectly honest, you undoubtedly will encounter some low points during your own rhetorical experiments, when your soul seems stubbornly unbent. You might feel that way right now, having encountered a set of persuasive tools without a sufficiently compelling reason to use them. I'm hoping that you found some helpful tips for making small changes, such as getting yourself to exercise more or drink less; but what about the big change: your own grand Hyperbole and the hot pursuit of happiness?

Throughout this book we've covered ways to understand your soul, convert it into an audience, and wield various rhetorical tools to bend it. Now it's time to pull things together. The Greeks believed that every tale should end in a moral and every speech in a peroration—a heart-pounding climax that nails home all the points you've made. Perorations and story morals serve much the same purpose: ending things with a bang and telling you what it all means. Some Greeks believed the same principle applies to our experience of life. The philosopher Solon famously said that one cannot tell the nature of a person's life until death. Aristotle agreed. A great tragedy ends with the character dying honorably, expressing his noble soul right to the end. Think Braveheart yelling, "Freedom!" right before his execution. Or the dying Captain Miller telling Private Ryan, "Earn this." It gives all the action a higher purpose.

When the poet Dylan Thomas was a young boy, he received a book that told him "everything about the wasp except why." You have met the tools. Now let's talk about the *why*—not just of self-improvement but of life itself.

This is the part in any inspirational book where the author

asks, "So what's your purpose?" I won't be doing that. Aristotle believed you don't have to look for your purpose. You already have it, within your own soul. In the previous chapters, we saw ways to know that soul—separate its meaningful needs from your daily self's appetites, and to bend it into accepting your worthy ethos. Your purpose lies within this practice of *psychagogia*, or soul bending. And here you'll find a kind of recursive magic. Every salesperson will tell you that when he applies his skill to a customer or client, he finds himself believing more in what he's selling. His manipulation splashes back onto himself.

Self-persuasion works the same way. When you bend your soul, you bend yourself. The grander the goal you set for yourself—the more ambitious the Hyperbole—the more you might find the deepest happiness. That's because your Aristotelian soul contains the meaning of your life.

Our modern attempts at self-improvement fail when we bypass the soul. While corporate workshops feature inspiring stories of the "purposeful life"—who could possibly be against that?—something is missing in that all-inclusive concept. It's the *why* without the wasp, a purpose without meaning, a desire without the soul's true need.

A typical self-improvement workshop often includes the tale of the three bricklayers. It's the "Freebird" of keynote speeches. You may have heard it:

A builder in need of a bricklayer is walking down the street when he sees three men working on a big church project. He asks the first man what he's doing.

"I'm laying bricks," the man answers, showing saintly patience with the stupid question.

The builder asks the same question of the second bricklayer. "I'm earning a living and providing for my family," he says.

The third man delivers the inspiring punch line: "I'm building a cathedral!"

That bricklayer has *purpose*, see. The builder is supposed to hire him because he will show up for work raring to go—knowing he isn't just laying bricks but, with Elon Musk–level motivation, building sacred castles. (The story never mentions why the man would leave a cathedral to work for the builder, but we won't go there.)

Would Aristotle hire the cathedral-making bricklayer? I doubt it. Assuming he supplemented his philosophy income with a construction business, Aristotle most likely would focus on the first worker, the one who was simply laying bricks. Was the man absorbed in what he was doing? Did he seem proud of his hand-eye coordination? If so, perhaps bricklaying paired beautifully with the man's precision-aligned soul.

The second bricklayer, concerned with providing for his family, would doubtless quit for a higher-paying line of work. And Cathedral Guy? Maybe he has the soul of a stonemason and should be carving weird gargoyles instead of laying bricks. Or his soul inclines him more toward architecture or, who knows, the priesthood. Aristotle would look for a bricklayer with a bricklaying soul. That man would be not just the best bricklayer but also the most soulful—and therefore the most human.

Well, what is especially human about linking our lives to our souls? What makes our species any more soulful than an albatross or a cockroach, those undaunted explorers of sea and darkness?

This is not a rhetorical question.

If we were having this discussion with Socrates, the man would beam at us and say, "Being more human . . . what an interesting concept! Now, please define *human*." As usually happens with that aggravating philosopher, we would find ourselves humbled. Socrates would doubtless steer us to compare ourselves with other creatures. And rightly so. Nearly all the distinctions that make us proud to be card-carrying members of the *Homo* genus have turned out to be skills exhibited by other creatures.

Tool use, for instance. Zoologists keep finding more species that manipulate objects to gather food or make new things.

What about building? A pair of beavers can throw together a quarter-mile-long dam in less than a week, and termites mastered air-conditioning towers a few million years ago. Beat that, bricklayer!

Art? Show me a spider's web that isn't uniquely, even creatively beautiful. The Antarctic krill, *Euphausia superba* ("beautiful illumination"), boasts a bioluminescent display that our pathetic three-color retinas can only begin to appreciate. Oh, sure, maybe we humans can grasp that beauty better than these poor dumb creatures. But that aesthetic reflex likely evolved from some primitive sense of satisfaction, the sort a spider just may get from a well-ordered web.

Cooperation? Watch a murmuration of starlings; or that Antarctic krill, whose flashing light signals allow hundreds of thousands of half-inch shrimp to switch direction instantly.

Maybe we're the most adaptable species? Tell that to any self-respecting rat or cockroach.

Play? Deception? Sexual variation? Please. An honest comparison of any of our traits with the rest of the animal kingdom makes us seem second-rate.

Except for one thing: words. Words make us human. They separate our species from any other and make us uniquely aware of our souls. Of all the creatures on earth, we are the ones with the stories, the animals who seek meaning. Through words we can erase time and discover what Aristotle was thinking thousands of years ago. We can erase space, seeing inside the minds of people unlike ourselves. Our disciplined use of words has helped us grasp the intentions of beavers and shrimp. We can convey abstractions and manipulate them at will. With our trope-forward thinking, we can find likenesses even among abstractions, allowing us to invent democracy and iPhones. Words encode our thoughts and spread them abroad.

Most important, Aristotle would say, words let us bend our souls. Without words, we just wouldn't be human. The more we tap into their power, the more human we are. And the more human we are, the happier we find ourselves. This is why the ancients valued rhetoric, the art that taps the power of words, above all other education.

In ancient times, words lay at the center of everything. Oration, poetry, and plays formed the greatest entertainment other than sport. And arguing itself counted as a kind of sport. The Greeks loved to debate. I imagine Cynics, Skeptics, Stoics, Academicians, Epicureans, and unaffiliated conversationalists going at it like gangbusters, maybe switching affiliations just for the sake of argument. They didn't argue over "purpose." They focused on how to get to the good life, through virtue or good habits or a particular state of mind. None of them strayed too far from one central point of agreement:

The greatest happiness comes from being the most human.

Aristotle wrote that the secret of the good life, the happiest life, is to be as human as humanly possible. This meant aligning oneself with one's noble and virtuous soul. The end, as the previous chapters tried to show, is not self-help but self-*mastery.* That is how we free ourselves from fears, lack of motivation, and bad habits. And our masterful use of words—with ourselves as well as with one another—leads to self-mastery.

You and I live in an especially good time to study freedom and being human. We're already feeling the first drops of the AI tempest, as software and robots eliminate jobs in tech and other fields. But in the short term at least, our problem may not be computers but us. The threat lies in our abandonment of studying how to be human. That is what this peroration is about. And it's the moral of the story of rhetoric.

We can't know our purpose without words. Yet it seems that our culture often leads young people in the opposite direction. We have come to fear words. School boards and entire states ban books from school libraries. We're even beginning to outsource our writing to AI's large language models. Worst of all, we're succumbing to the black magic of rhetoric instead of learning its charms.

So this is the moral to my argument, and the ultimate *why* of my mountainous venture. I hope you find yourself inspired to try your own rhetorical experiments and discover your deepest word-centric humanity. You just might feel inspired to share its magic with kids and parents, spreading the civilizing gospel of the power of words. Sharing the happiness that comes from being the most human.

And then, after we bend our souls and change ourselves, we can change the world.

The Tools

Soul

Aristotle described the ideal soul as a "noble" one. While ancient Greeks believed we inherit soulful traits from our ancestors, the philosopher clearly thought we have some responsibility over the matter. His noble soul is:

Just: acting fairly at all times, like a good judge.

Courageous: brave but not foolhardy.

Restrained: Your rational side controls your emotions.

Magnanimous: generous, not to win approval but because you really care.

Liberal: free from the constraints of power or other people's judgment.

Prudent: taking the middle course in major decisions.

Wise: curious, knowledgeable, and streetwise as well as educated.

Soul Detector

Discover the characteristics of your very own soul with these exercises:

1. Think when you acted nobly. What motivated you? See Aristotle's definition of the noble soul. Were you especially courageous? Magnanimous? Wise? Do you see a pattern of nobility?

2. Recall the times when you acted shamefully. What embarrassed you?

3. Think when you suffered outrageous fortune. How did you respond?

4. Separate your wants—Aristotle called them appetites—from your soul's true needs. Take stock of your expenses. Imagine cutting your household budget in half. What would you eliminate? This doesn't mean wearing sackcloth and eating porridge. It's just an exercise to find the outline of your soul. In fact, you may find more of your truest needs when

you restore the other half of your budget. How would you spend differently?

Decorum

The word is Latin for "fitness," as in fitting with your social environment. The trick to fitting in with your soul is to see it as a loving person who watches over you. Your soul wants you to behave. This can make for an extremely annoying doppelgänger. But your soul knows it's good for you.

Ethos

Aristotle described ethos as people's impression of your character. A corporate brand is an ethos that can be worth billions. Your individual ethos—your reputation—has value all its own. To persuade yourself into better habits, and motivate yourself to achieve your goals, you want to try and make a good impression on your soul. Aristotle listed three characteristics of a worthy ethos: *eunoia* (disinterest), *phronesis* (practical wisdom), and *arete* (virtue). We can call them Caring, Craft, and Cause.

> *Caring.* You make your soul believe you have its best interest at heart. This means practicing **philos**, the Greeks' lavish sense of loyalty.
>
> *Craft.* You prove to your soul that you have the knowledge and smarts to solve the problem at hand. But we're talking rhetoric here, not scientific proof. In convincing your soul that you know what you're doing, you end up convincing yourself. (See *Confidence* below.)

Cause. The ancient Greeks and Romans believed that Cause, or virtue, is exclusive to men. (The Latin *virtus* comes from the word *vir,* meaning "man.") That's because women had little agency in those days. In our time, we all can try to live up to our souls' nobility. The trick is to free ourselves from our appetites when they interfere with our souls' needs. (See *Soul,* above, for a list of noble traits.) One way to demonstrate your Cause is to have a cause—a noble goal. (See *Hyperbole.*)

Sin recovery. To keep yourself from being mired in guilt, you can view the sin as a temporary lapse. In fact, your sense of shame reveals a good soul. Allow that soul to forgive you. (See *Philos.*)

Emotions

The Greeks believed that the quest for a good life means a struggle between the rational and "pathetic" sides of our characters. *Logos,* logic, should take the upper hand over *pathos,* or feelings. Aristotle realized that our "sorry human nature" tends to give pathos the upper hand. When it comes to self-persuasion, though, emotions offer us some of the best manipulative tools. Below you'll find the emotions that have the most persuasive power. But remember that the good life, Aristotle-style, is all about balance. This counts especially when it comes to the emotions. Fear is bad, but a prudent soul holds itself back from foolhardiness. Shame can be crippling, but too much envy can get you in trouble. Balance fear and foolhardiness, and you get courage.

Confidence comes from a feeling of power and control. You want to believe yourself to be strong, rich, and popular. So what if you happen to be a poor, lonely weakling? Your problem is rhetorical, not circumstantial. Strength, wealth, and popularity are all open to definition. You may be weak in body but strong in courage. Wealth depends on meeting your needs rather than delighting in meeting your appetites. And, given the right attitude, anyone who owns a good dog can consider herself popular. (See *Framing*.)

Shame makes a great soul detector. If you embarrass yourself when alone, that's your soul raising a virtuous eyebrow over your ignoble behavior. Don't mistake shame for guilt. While guilt has to do with past sins, shame is a temporary emotion. It keeps you on your virtuous toes.

Fear, Aristotle said, is another temporary emotion. In modern terms, a lasting sense of fear may be a sign of neurosis. Otherwise, face your fears by evaluating the particular danger and calculating the odds. Call this a fear lens. It uses your rational side to tamp down the emotion.

Envy can be a positive emotion. Use it to enhance your competitiveness. Remember that you can be envious of your own irritating soul.

Laughter's tool is mild, forgiving self-deprecation. This shouldn't make you less confident. Instead, it brings your intimidating soul down to size. Forgive your temporary lapses, and see them as goofs. Laugh at them and move on.

Desire is all about timing. (See *Kairos*.) Separate your long-term desires from your temporary appetites. Now make those goals seem immediate. When you see a donut, envision your future smaller waist size. It can help you skip the donut.

Charm is the magic that comes from what Plato called "sweet words." (See *Charms*.) In ancient times, charms were magical expressions on amulets or medals. In modern medicine, the "charm" of a drug has to do with its placebo effect. Aristotle believed that you can turn yourself into a charm. He called this ability *karisma*. To see yourself as charismatic, rewrite your résumé or type up a flattering biography. It's a placebo for your soul.

Catharsis, a method of emotional purification, can help balance our mood—especially when we're feeling too much self-pity and fear. Listen to heartbreak songs or watch a sad movie, and you might experience the balanced mood that Aristotle called "cathartic pleasure." Mood restored.

Cognitive ease. Aristotle called it "receptivity," the kind of mood that leaves you open to persuasion. Modern behavioral scientists report that your brain uses relatively little energy in this state. You become more Homer Simpson than Stephen Hawking. To get into this state, you need to smile, relax, and manage to feel in control. Don't feel this makes you stupid. See it as turning yourself into your own best soulful audience. But skip the donut. You're not Homer Simpson.

Logic

While Aristotle believed that ethos outweighs logos in persuading an audience, our rational side has its uses. In rhetoric, though, logic works somewhat differently from the formal version. A good fallacy can come in handy. A successful proof can result from a mere belief. And framing may count as the most powerful logos tool of all.

Induction. This branch of logic collects evidence to reach a conclusion. It can help you tell a convincing tale (see *Story*) while avoiding the paralyzing mood that results from doomscrolling. The inductive process works through four questions:

> What is it?
> What caused it?
> Why?
> Is it a trend?

Enthymeme. Aristotle invented this tool for rhetorical deduction. While induction reaches a conclusion only after uncovering the evidence, deduction starts with a fact or belief and applies it to the particular situation. The enthymeme has just two parts: the proof and the conclusion. Pigs don't have wings, therefore they don't fly. The enthymeme can be useful in boosting your confidence. Make your proof a positive one: *I'm a good learner, so I can do this new job.* (See *Framing.*)

Framing. What mood is to pathos, framing is to logos. The frame eases a disagreement or choice, lubricating an issue to make it work your way. Three framing tools help you turn the argument in your head into successful persuasion.

Broaden the issue. Getting up early is about carving out an hour just for myself.

> ***Redefine the terms.*** Turn *pain* into a *test of my ability to suffer.* Or euphemize the hard stuff. *Running? I'm just stretching my legs.*
>
> ***Focus.*** Simplify and personalize. *Dance lessons are about performing a perfect swing at my wedding.*
>
> ***Deliberative rhetoric.*** The language of decisions, according to Aristotle. Deliberative rhetoric focuses on the future, allowing you to move beyond the guilt or nostalgia of the past and present-tense labels for what a horrible person you are. When you think of the future, think choices, not just threats; you'll give yourself a renewed sense of agency.

Habits

"Character," Plutarch said, "is simply habit long continued." He was following Aristotle's wisdom that happiness comes from habituation. Habits save us mental energy by removing choices, putting parts of our lives on autopilot. If you always floss at night, that habit keeps you from standing in the bathroom debating whether you really want to take the trouble. Of course, bad habits remove choices as much as good habits do. The trick to acquiring a good habit is to ease into it.

> ***Lure & Ramp.*** To talk an audience, including yourself, into taking an action, make the goal seem magnificent and the effort appear easy. First, focus on the goal with all the optimism you can muster. Then chunk the steps into relatively easy actions.

Tortoise Method. This tool applies the Lure & Ramp to establishing a new habit. Start by thinking of the habit as something you do for your soul. (See *Philos.*) Next, set a generous timeline. Don't expect to perfect the habit in a day or a week. Think in terms of months, years, or even a lifetime. Proceed modestly.

Personal time zone. New habits often get stymied by our lack of time. Carve out an hour or two from a time of day you don't use well. This could mean going to bed early rather than streaming videos for an extra hour, or taking a midday nap instead of buying lunch. If all this seems daunting, impossible, or just plain crazy, reframe the idea this way: We all need to seize any opportunity to own our time. (See *Kairos.*)

Figures and Tropes

Any use of language that strays from the same old normal or literal is probably either a figure or a trope. A figure renders an expression with unusual words or patterns. Its novelty or rhythm can make it sticky, forming an earworm in your mind. Repeat it often enough and it can even form a charm, working the magic of belief in a goal—or in yourself. Tropes take the magic up a notch by shifting reality. The Sophists believed that figures and tropes bend the soul.

Figures

Paean. A rhythmic chant that plays with short and long syllables. *Repel them, repel, them, make them relinquish the ball!* Ancient soldiers used paeans as war chants called *slogans.* Modern advertising slogans use rhythmic figures to stick in our heads and foster profitable addictions: *Betcha can't eat just one.* If you need a self-motivating expression, borrow a Madison Avenue rhythm or play with short and long syllables. *First the nutrition, then the junk.*

Tropes

Analogical thinking lies behind most tropes. This habit of mind starts with the belief that everything is connected. You can use this habit to reframe your skill set and boost your confidence. Your ability to arrange your books shows that you can understand high-level concepts. Your perseverance with a jigsaw puzzle proves you can stick to any task.

Metaphor takes two things that share a characteristic and presents that one thing as the other. The moon is round like a balloon, so the moon *is* a balloon. War is an attack of one group on another; this government policy "attacks" the middle class; therefore, this policy wages war on the middle class! Aristotle believed that the most vivid kind of metaphor contains a dose of the unexpected. The more unlikely the comparison, the better. Computer nerds came up with the metaphor *jailbreak* to refer to the use of unauthorized apps on a smartphone. Rewriting a few lines of code doesn't seem exactly equivalent to escaping from a prison, but the term makes metaphorical sense. You can use the trope to break out of your own routines. An evening jog can turn into an "escape." Doing a budget can become "numerical storytelling." Hey, if it makes you smile, you make your day that much better. (See *Cognitive ease.*)

Irony says one thing while meaning the opposite. Nature and human interactions are full of ironic devices. *Oh, you shouldn't have!* Strangely, irony can help you ease the way into a more positive attitude. Start by speaking ironically about an excruciating task: *It was . . . fun!* Then repeat it so often it no longer seems ironic. Self-persuasion often means using tools or expressions that make you cringe at first. Start by using them ironically, and gradually make them true. Not every trope has to remain a trope.

Synecdoche takes a representative sample and turns it into the whole thing. A lower-body workout is "leg day." Sitting down to write a proposal is "creative sitting."

Metonymy takes a characteristic, container, or action and, like the synecdoche, makes it stand for the whole thing. A smart kid is a "brain." Traveling to another town is "hitting the road."

Pidgin thinking. Pidgin dialects use metonymy to create memorable expressions. *Why strong face?* A great way to coin your own metonymy is to use "pidgin thinking," simplifying a concept to its bare essentials. First, find the essential elements. *Potato chips are discs that expand the belly.* Next, explore contiguities—seemingly unlike things that belong together. *Chips go in, belly out.*

Charms. In rhetoric, charms are figures of speech, repeated often enough until they bend the soul. (See *Figures, Repetition.*)

Repetition. By repeating a charm over and over, you can seal your belief in the expression, however dubious it might be in reality.

Hyperbole

This astonishing device belongs to the tropes, but it works so many wonders that it deserves its very own category of persuasion. It's hard to imagine this expansive trope without adding a capital *H* to it. When we do that, we just might find ourselves creating a dreamlike goal that throws beyond our daily reality. (The term itself comes from the Greek for "throw beyond.")

A great Hyperbole (and every true Hyperbole is great by definition) boasts these elements.

- The goal seems slightly beyond the possible.
- It entails some risk, if only of embarrassment.
- The work, and the eventual outcome, seem compellingly novel.
- Ideally, the accomplishment should be a first of some sort, something that (technically, seen in the right light) no one has ever done before.
- For more drama, the effort can lead to a climactic moment of some sort—a birthday, a wedding, a countdown, whatever.
- Overall, the task should make you better off even if you fail. You end up fitter, or more skillful, or happier.

Time (Kairos)

Kairos is the art of opportunity, the ability to navigate through the chaos of life. If the notion confuses you—how can you see the whirlpool of chaos as an open door?—watch Kansas City quarterback Patrick Mahomes. Where another player might see nothing but a stampede of giant men bent on destroying him and his receivers, Mahomes sees openings. He's a genius at mapping what the Greeks called *khaos*. Which means "gap."

Gap mapping. Envision the messy parts of life geographically. Draw a mind map of a particularly chaotic time—work, evening, vacation—by showing the sources of trouble as objects. Draw a terrain, with the strongest forces on the hills. Find a path between them.

Chaotic reframing. This starts by reframing yourself as a kairoticist, someone willing to leave the comfort zone and explore the gaps caused by change. Chaos can be a threat, or an interesting problem, or a place to explore and maybe even settle in.

Exigence. Write down your problem as specifically as possible, then rewrite it until the editing itself forms an idea.

Nostalgia cure. When you miss the good old days to the point where you hate the present, you can legitimately consider nostalgia to be a disease. It's a relatively mild disease, one involving baby pictures and discontinued candy you can still buy online, but a disease nonetheless. When we think the world should return to some mythical, idyllic former state, then nostalgia becomes a social disease that makes us retreat from the chaos. A cure lies in realistic memory. Aristotle said to remember the bad times as well as the good, thinking about how you responded to those times. Your actions revealed your soul. Next, create things to look forward to. Finally, during times of stress, focus on what you actually want. What's your true goal?

Story

Learn to tell a heroic tale and you can turn yourself into a hero. A good yarn is worth a thousand embarrassing facts about you. Here, again, Aristotle tells us how.

> *Connected events.* Most of us tell and-then stories, simply listing each action. Aristotle knew that the most compelling tales connect each action to the next by making one cause the other.
>
> *Tying and untying.* The best way to connect events is to show them as a series of problems that the hero (you) must solve. Aristotle called this technique tying (*desis*) and untying (*lusis*). Each solution leads to, or causes, another problem. The result is a story that seems inevitable while building sympathy for the hero. It's how you convince your soul that your daily self is worthy.
>
> *Hero's journey.* This time-honored method of tale telling starts with the main character (you again!) leaving her comfort zone and going on a quest. She overcomes a set of obstacles, reaches a moment of near-certain defeat, joins up with allies, and triumphs in the end. Each scene leads to the next one as the hero unties one narrative knot, only to find another. The hero's journey offers an easy way to plot your own goal. Write the story, then try to make it heroically come true.
>
> *Beats.* Screenwriters use the beat system for just about every hit movie. It follows Aristotle's rule that a play must

contain three acts. In the Save the Cat system, a plot also contains five "foundation" beats:

Catalyst. An inciting incident or life-changing event that forces the hero out of his comfort zone. If you happen to be the hero, think of a particular moment that represents the problem you most want to solve, or the chaos you need to find your way through.

Break into Two. The second act begins with our hero accepting the call to commit to a goal.

Midpoint. Usually a false victory. The hero seems to untie the big problem.

All Is Lost. Immediately after the Midpoint, the world collapses around the hero. The problem has not been solved after all. The beauty of this beat is that it turns your own defeat into a plot point. You can make yourself believe that the story won't end there.

Break into Three. Act 3, that is. The ultimate problem gets solved, the hero triumphs, and the bigger lesson gets learned. That lesson may be that what seems like a failure—you came short of the goal—counts as a kind of success. The effort itself has been good for your soul.

Inspiration

If you struggle to come up with a brilliant solution to a problem, or just find yourself lacking any creativity, reframe the very idea of inspiration. Think of it not as some genetic gift but as a set of methods. Tech engineers say they "prompt" AI algorithms. It's a good way to think about these tools. See them as ways to prompt your own inspiration.

Compounding. Combine two existing ideas to create a new one—a kind of thought molecule.

Modeling. Write a tale about your future self. (See *Story.*) Make up a series of problems and obstacles, and show yourself untying them. You're doing what a computer model does: generating a future. You "train" your story by describing your own character, revealing your soul through the actions you would most likely take.

Refinement. Take an existing idea and revise it. Or improve your self-impression by writing a detailed description, then rewriting it until it seems admirable. You've learned something new and inspiring about yourself.

Failure. While this hardly seems a tool, it can become a great source of inspiration. Some of the best inventions—potato chips, Post-it notes—have come from mistakes. Reframe your failures, not just as lessons but as problems for you to untie.

Liberality. Reframe the chaos in your life, seeing any change as an interesting problem rather than a threat. In doing this, you free yourself from paralyzing fear.

Further Reading

"It is the mark of an educated mind to be able to entertain a thought without accepting it."

—Aristotle, *Metaphysics*

"A fox knows many things," the philosopher Archilochus said, "but a hedgehog knows one big thing." Scholars are hedgehogs. They spend their careers seeking to know their one big thing, usually a narrow subdiscipline that offers a glimpse at a cross section of the universe. Journalists like me are foxes, sniffing around human rabbit holes in hope of something juicy. Even when we specialize in something—in my case, classical rhetoric—we don't really research. We just read a lot and then bother the scholarly hedgehogs with questions. While wise people throughout the ages have rightly admired the deeply knowing hedgehog, I've found that an intellectually curious journalist tends to be happier than your average scholar.

This rather scattershot list, a sampling of the dozens of books that informed this one, is for foxes, not your classically trained hedgehogs. Sniff around and see what comes up; then hare after whatever pleases. Michel de Montaigne, who clearly placed himself far on the fox end of the fox–hedgehog spectrum, said that when he tired of one book, he simply dropped it and picked up another. No self-respecting scholar would do that. But Montaigne was, famously, a happy man.

Rhetoric

About thirty years ago, when I first became interested in the art of persuasion, I looked for a fun, readable book on rhetoric. The textbooks I found were disappointingly dry and humorless. This was rhetoric, for crying out loud! Wasn't it supposed to seduce me? So, after some years of poring over Aristotle, Isocrates, Quintilian, and Cicero, and bothering rhetoricians around the world, I wrote my own book, *Thank You for Arguing*. It continues to serve as the leading primer on rhetoric, at least in terms of copies sold and students assigned. As obnoxious as it seems to recommend my own book, my motives for writing it were pure.

Books published later on the subject cover sharper angles. *Good Arguments* covers the elements of debating. Written by Bo Seo, a champion debater who now teaches at Harvard, it's a good yarn as well as an informative book about that aspect of rhetoric. Look up books covered under Debate, and you'll find other worthy texts. But they tend to be hedgehoggish, covering one big thing rather than the broad spectrum that rhetoric offers.

If you want to view the whole sweep of the art, see if your library has the *Encyclopedia of Rhetoric*. Edited by Thomas O. Sloane and published in 2001 by the Oxford University Press, this eight-hundred-plus-page tome contains articles by leading scholars covering classical rhetoric, modern rhetoric, and all rhetorical things in between. A new copy will set you back about $200.

Aristotle

The problem with reading the greatest philosopher of all time, the man who literally wrote the book on rhetoric, is that Aristotle makes for terrible reading. Many scholars believe that he never really wrote for publication but instead scribbled voluminous lecture notes. So, if you happen to be an Aristotle rookie, get an introduction by the late University of Chicago philosopher Mortimer Adler. His *Aristotle for Everybody* offers a neat summary of the philosopher's thinking. Skipping Aristotle's work on the natural sciences and medicine, Adler focuses on his logical theories, along with his exploration of happiness. Mind you, Adler is no laugh riot. His book reads like an Aristotle 101 course taught by a stern but deeply knowledgeable professor. Still, it's the best introduction you can get without an actual teacher.

Having taken your dose of Adler, you will be ready to read Aristotle himself. I found *On the Soul* to be his most entertaining work. (Remember, you have to set a low bar for fun here. Aristotle can be exhilarating, the same way an agonizing climb up a scree-covered mountain can be exhilarating.) His *Nicomachean Ethics* offers his best writing on happiness. Movie screenwriters continue to worship his *Poetics*, a manual on holding an audience's attention and making them cry. And his *Rhetoric*, of course, is a must-read for anyone who wants to tackle the foundational book on the art.

While all of his writing can be found for free on the Web, you might want the revised Oxford translation of *The Complete Works of Aristotle*—published not by Oxford but by the Princeton University Press. The two volumes cost more than a hundred dollars, but any good library should have it. Originally published in twelve volumes between 1912 and 1951, *The Complete Works* counts as one of the great feats of classical scholarship. The book may be worth the expense if you care to see someone's eyebrows rise at the sight of it in your home. Tell them, "It counts as one of the great feats of classical scholarship."

Sophists

W.K.C. Guthrie's *The Sophists* offers the best primer on Gorgias and his fellow itinerant orator-teachers. As for Gorgias himself, you would expect that he wrote some blockbuster books, and he apparently did. Alas, little survives. But his *Encomium of Helen*, a forensic defense of the woman who launched the thousand ships, can be found online today in various translations. It is everything you would expect from this oratorical version of an ancient rock star. (By "ancient rock star," I mean a celebrity who lived a millennium or two ago, not Mick Jagger.)

Susan C. Jarratt offers a good scholarly defense of these much maligned manipulators in *Rereading the Sophists: Classical Rhetoric Refigured*. If you want to make up your own mind about them, read the original Sophist works in the Penguin Classics edition of *The Greek Sophists,* edited and with an introduction by John Dillon and Tania Gergel. To see how sophistry found its way into philosophy, look into *Protagoras* by Daniel Silvermintz. One of the original Sophists, Protagoras helped create sophistic philosophy. He came up with the most controversial philosophical sentence ever written: "Of all things the measure is Man, of the things that are, that they are, and of the things that are not, that they are not." Believing that every person bears a separate truth, Protagoras lit the first spark of what today we call humanism.

Cicero

After Aristotle, Cicero counts as the greatest of classical rhetoricians. He wrote several books on rhetoric, mostly in dialogue form. Cicero occasionally described himself as a Stoic, but his actions as Rome's most famous consul show anything but a stoical attitude. Anthony Everitt's *Cicero: The Life and Times of Rome's Greatest Politician* tells the best story of one of history's great characters. Someone should make a movie of this man, with Gary Oldman in the lead.

For Cicero's own work, there's *On the Orator*, a readable textbook published by the Loeb Classical Library. While you can find various translations online for free, the version translated by E. W. Sutton and H. Rackham seems the most reliable. And don't miss Cicero's *Selected Letters,* published by Penguin Classics. Much of what we understand about ancient Rome starts with Cicero's letters to his brother and friends. The man comes off as funny, catty, biting, and brilliant. After struggling to swallow Aristotle, cleanse the palate with Cicero's letters.

Stoicism

To be honest, I haven't spent a great deal of time with the Stoics. Their virtuous philosophy does not appeal. But one of the greatest Stoics, Epictetus, wrote readable lectures on the subject. At a secondhand book sale, I bought a small volume, *Discourses of Epictetus,* translated by T. W. Rolleston. You can find it for free on the Web. It's worth browsing for the notes in the back, defining the terms that Epictetus used—a complete lexicography of Stoicism.

It seems a mystery that anyone could truly live as a Stoic without lapsing into unstoical hypocrisy. Emily Wilson's *Seneca: A Life* describes just such a hypocrite while offering a clear look at the philosophy itself. Seneca, a superb writer, philosopher, and Roman éminence grise, advised Nero, reluctantly sucking up to the monstrous emperor until he was accused of joining an assassination plot and was forced to commit suicide. It's the most Roman of Roman stories. (Since writing that book, Wilson struck literary gold with her fresh translations of Homer's *Odyssey* and *Iliad*.)

Epicureanism

Few of Epicurus's writings have survived. What's left can be found in *The Art of Happiness*, translated by George K. Strodach, who also provided an introduction and commentary. The book adds notes about Epicurus by ancient Romans. If you find happiness in reading turgid, preachy texts, don't miss this one.

If that fails to bring you joy, head straight to Lucretius, *The Nature of Things*, translated by A. E. Stallings, with an excellent introduction by Oxford classicist Richard Jenkyns. Stallings uses rhyming couplets to give the modern reader the feeling that scholars get from the original Latin. Titus Lucretius Carus was a Roman who chose to explain Epicureanism through poetry; as he put it, poetry sweetens the bitter medicine of philosophy the way a doctor adds honey to a cup of wormwood to get a child to drink it. You really should not pass this one up. Here's a taste. To explain why the soul is made up of atoms that disperse when the person dies, he writes:

> *And another thing: when wine has soaked a fellow to the core,*
> *And through his veins has scattered and distributed its heat,*
> *Why do his limbs grow leaden, why does he trip*
> *on his own feet?*

> *Why does his mind sop, his sight swim, his tongue drawl?*
> *Why does he burst with bellowing, and belching and a brawl,*
> *And all the usual things that follow on a drunken spree?*
> *Why, indeed, unless the wine's ferocity*
> *Tends to disrupt the spirit even while it's in the frame.*
> *It's clear that if a thing can be disrupted, then the same,*
> *If penetrated by the force of slightly stronger sway,*
> *Will be deprived of any future and will pass away.*

All that to explain atomic theory. Such honey!

Magic and Charms

For the charms themselves, you'll find no better guide than Richard A. Lanham's *A Handlist of Rhetorical Terms*. The rhetorician defines all the tropes and major figures of speech and thought (along with some delightful minor terms), with examples from literature.

A wonderful website, Silva Rhetoricae: The Forest of Rhetoric (rhetoric.byu.edu), offers a tour through the ancient art while defining the terms.

For the magic part, see *Magic and Rhetoric in Ancient Greece*, published by the Harvard University Press. This slim volume comprises four lectures delivered by the groundbreaking French scholar Jacqueline de Romilly at Harvard in 1974. You'll need to print out the Greek alphabet to understand her terms. But I found de Romilly's take on Greek magic to be vastly informative; I almost said magical.

Humanism and the Humanities

Sarah Bakewell's *Humanly Possible* covers humanism and its characters through history. Bakewell happens to be one of those rare academics who can write a gripping story while explaining complex philosophy. She boils humanism's essence down to four principles: universality, diversity, critical thinking, and moral connection. In explaining Quintilian's debatable notion that true rhetoric requires a virtuous speaker, Bakewell writes:

> Thus, to use language well is about more than adding decorative twiddles; it is about moving other people to emotion and recognition. It is a moral activity, because being able to communicate well is at the heart of *humanitas*—of being human in the fullest way.

If you're concerned about our future AI overlords, read this book. And for that matter, read anything by Bakewell. Her biography of Montaigne, *How to Live*, tells the story of history's happiest man while offering a how-to guide to happiness.

Then again, Montaigne's *The Complete Essays,* translated by M. A. Screech, are thoroughly enjoyable on their own. Read the essays the way Montaigne himself certainly would, dipping into the ones with the most intriguing titles ("On the Cannibals," "On Fleeing from Pleasures at the Cost of One's Life," "How Our Mind Tangles Itself Up," "To Philosophize Is to Learn How to Die"). You quickly discover that Montaigne has an ADHD tendency to forget the titles of his essays while writing them. But you find yourself just going with his humanistic flow. How I love this man.

Storytelling

The "beats" system, described by the screenwriter Blake Snyder in *Save the Cat*, offers a delightful way to outline your story. But you might skip Snyder and go straight to Jessica Brody's *Save the Cat*

Writes a Novel. It boils the fifteen beats of *Save the Cat* down to the essential five. Get the beats, and you have a story. This applies to the tale you can tell about your future self.

Happiness

The scholar Garry Wills wrote the single best description of the eighteenth-century humanists' take on humanism in his book *Inventing America.* Why should you care? Because our modern idea of happiness owes much to Thomas Jefferson and the British humanists he studied.

For the rest of your happiness reading, see the other books recommended in this section. All of them, even the ones about Stoicism, can eventually lead to your own happiness.

Words

The Oxford English Dictionary has been a major player in this book, and for good reason. Unlike any dictionary that came before, the *OED* leads with the belief that all our words—and the entire history of those words—should be available to everyone. Before the *OED,* dictionary writers illiberally intended their work to fix the language in place. Any word that they excluded, or any definition that strayed from the dictionary's version, would be "improper." Early dictionaries separated right from wrong and divided the right-thinking sorts from the hoi polloi. The French still have their Academy of the Forty, whose noble task is to maintain the purity of their language. The Germans and Italians have their own versions of august lexicon keepers. The founders of the *OED* had a radically different idea. English, they realized, could not possibly be fixed. It changes, it evolves. A word's meaning strays from mouth to mouth.

By printing the biography of every English word, the *OED* would help readers understand the history of thought in its minutest detail. It was the greatest lexicographical capital-H Hyperbole ever.

To learn the full wonderful story of the *OED*, read *The Professor and the Madman: A Tale of Murder, Insanity, and the Making of the Oxford English Dictionary* by Simon Winchester. It got made into a so-so film starring Mel Gibson and Sean Penn; get the book instead. Winchester notes that the *OED* saw its first full publication in 1928, eighty-four years after Britain's Philological Society first proposed it. The genius of the dictionary would be its reliance on published quotations. It wouldn't prescribe "proper" meanings but would apply inductive logic to the task, extracting each word's definitions from previous use. Thousands of volunteers and dozens of researchers delved into English usage, tracing its origins back to Anglo Saxon and ancient Greek. J.R.R. Tolkien was one young employee; eighteen years before writing *The Hobbit*, he worked on the etymologies of *waggle* through *warlock*.

The original plan was hugely ambitious: four volumes, 6,400 pages, in ten years. The actual effort took seventy-four years and totaled twelve volumes, including one supplement. Even before the lexicographers neared the finish line, they realized they had to stretch the goal even further. Culture changes. Scientific discoveries require new language. The dictionary originally left out the word *radium* on the basis that it was too obscure to be considered part of the English language. Several months later, Pierre and Marie Curie won the Nobel Prize for having discovered the element.

The dictionary's hyperbolic attempt—a vast tome compiling every known published use of every English word—had to be re-hyperbolized. (Yes, *hyperbolized* is in the *OED*.) A second edition, published in 1989, totaled 21,728 pages in twenty volumes. A third edition is in the works, with hopes of completion in the 2030s.

Needless to say, it will be vast. And even then, the work will have to continue if the *OED* will have any chance of seeming . . . what? Authoritative? Complete? Could it ever be?

Aristotle would understand. He knew that the world is anything but static. Life is contingent. But that hardly makes the *OED* meaningless. Our changing world makes it all the more important to understand what went before. And nothing offers us more insight into the minds of literate Anglo-Saxons. Renaissance poets, and pidgin speakers than the history of words and their uses. As Socrates knew, the single most important philosophical question is "What do you mean by . . ."

You can still buy a used compact 1971 edition of the dictionary, complete with magnifying glass. But first go to OED.com. This is one of the greatest websites ever created, with all the latest etymology, statistics on the frequency of a word's use over the centuries, and the kind of rabbit-hole etymology that lets you explore the English language as it meanders through individual minds. Full use requires a subscription, but your library should be able to give you access.

The biggest problem I have in looking up a word in the *OED* is that it leads me from related word to related word and their history and meanings and quotations, and an hour will go by, two hours, without my getting any work done, and I look up dizzy and zoned and . . . happy.

Acknowledgments

My favorite part of every televised award ceremony is when a celebrity tries to be humble while giving thanks. In every speech we see Aristotle's theories in living color: a soul revealed or carefully concealed, an ethos doing its best to show its philos toward the minions, and flickers of raw Aristotelian appetite in the lustful gaze at the statuette. *You never gave up on me!*

And now and then you find true humble gratitude, the kind I felt as I looked out from the summit of Mount Moosilauke, and that I'm feeling now.

Every author will tell you that reading multiple drafts of another person's book requires heroic patience and well-calibrated tact. My wife, Dorothy Behlen Heinrichs, sat with every appearance of interest as I read her the same passages, slightly revised, over and over. Talk about great acting. Her identical twin sister, Jane Masters, sometimes joined her, and even brought the wine.

Brilliant professional help came from Lee Michaelides, who

navigated neuroscience journals and critiqued my writing. Karen Sommerfeld gave the closest of all reads and corrected my errors large and small. Cynthia Cannell was the very first person to push me to write this book; and my literary agent, Brian DeFiore, made it possible. My editor at Crown, Matt Inman, was the kindest of coaches, setting me on course without a single harsh word.

Jim Collins and Kristen Laine provided their lakeside house, where I read Aristotle and the Sophists to the sound of calling loons. When it came to actually writing the book, I struggled right up to the moment when I boarded the Cunard Line's *Queen Mary 2* in the Brooklyn Harbor, bound for Southampton, England. For the next six days, I woke up at 4:30 A.M. Jaylight saving time (actually, ship time), and wrote until ten, pausing only to enjoy an English breakfast delivered each morning to my room. The rest of the day I was free to go out on deck, where I read Emily Wilson's entertaining translation of the *Odyssey*. I can't imagine a better writing retreat.

But my greatest thanks go to the hundreds of Advanced Placement English Language teachers who have allowed me to share my love of rhetoric. I chat with AP Lang classes several days a week, and every time, I get a question that stumps me. Teachers hold up our civilization and keep it going. They deserve our support and our deepest gratitude. And for what it's worth, they have mine.

Index

A
acting, 80–81
adaptability, 145–46
Adele, 105
adianoeta, 175
Aesion, 174
agency, 27, 44
Ali, Muhammad, 19
All Is Lost, 196–97, 200, 249
alliteration, 164–65
amygdala, 167
analogous/analogical thinking, 89, 137, 172–73, 244
Andreessen, Marc, 39–40
antecedent, fallacy of, 135–37
antilittering ad, 130–31

antithesis, 166
apatheia, 220
apathy, 220
Apollo program, 30
appeal to popularity, 138
appetite, 92–93, 101
arete (virtue), 19, 89
Aristotle
  on analogical thinking, 172–73
  author's deep dive into, 3–4
  on change, 27
  on chaos, 28
  on choice, 89, 143–44
  chunking and, 151–52
  on deduction, 115–18
  on defining terms, 126

Aristotle (*cont'd*):
  deliberative rhetoric and, 41–42
  on emotions, 94, 96, 98, 100, 101, 102, 103, 104
  on ethos, 81
  on fallacies, 139
  Fates and, 217, 219
  on friendship, 83–84
  further reading on, 253–54
  on happiness, 216, 217, 225
  on logos, 109–10
  on motivation, 92–93
  on narrative, 186–89, 192, 195–96, 200
  nostalgia and, 43
  on old people, 39, 43–44, 106
  opportunities and, 38
  on personhood, 112
  on pity, 133
  purpose and, 230, 231
  on reality, 110–11, 160, 168
  on receptivity, 94
  on rhetoric, 49
  on rhythmic language, 161
  soul, concept of, 4, 14, 16, 17, 128, 235–36
  on tropes, 174
  on wit, 6

Aronson, Elliot, 15
ataraxia (freedom from disturbance), 221–22
Atropos, 217
Aurelius, Marcus, 221

B

Babel, Isaac, 54
balance, 104–5
Barnum, P. T., 129–30
beats, 194–98, 200–201, 248–49
beliefs, 110–11, 118–21, 123, 160
Bezos, Jeff, 21
Birdseye, Clarence, 178–79
bookkeeping, double-entry, 49
Bradley, Milton, 30
Break into Three, 197–98, 200, 249
Break into Two, 195–96, 200, 249
broadening the issue, 130, 134, 241
Buddhism, 223, 226
Bush, George W., 181

C

cacodaimon, 218
Caesar, Julius, 100
camel, case of missing, 28–30

Caring, 83–85, 87, 90, 237
Carson, Rachel, 130
Catalyst, 195, 200, 249
catharsis, 104–6, 107, 240
cathartic pleasure, 105–6
Cause, 89–90, 91, 238
causes, induction and, 111–15
cave analogy, 53, 94, 128
celebrity worship syndrome, 180
change, times of, 31
change, navigating, 7–9
chaos, 26–28, 31–34, 37–40, 44, 247
charisma, 103–4
charm, 102–4, 107, 240
charms, 69, 158–84, 206, 245, 257
choice, 26, 30, 34–35, 39, 89, 109–10, 143–44, 219
chunking, 151–52, 181, 206
Cicero, Marcus Tullius, 19, 99, 163, 165, 221, 255
Clarkson, Kelly, 77
Clay, Cassius, 19
Clinton, Hillary, 187
Clotho, 216–17
Clytemnestra, 84–85
Cody, Iron Eyes, 131
cognitive dissonance, 15–16, 22, 80
cognitive ease, 94, 240
Comet Ping Pong, 187
commonplaces, 20–21, 37
compounding, 49, 58, 250
conception, idea as, 53
Concerning the Laughable, 100
confidence, 94–96, 106, 238–39
connection, narrative and, 187–92
contiguities, exploring, 179–80
Craft, 87–88, 91, 237
creative clearing, 35
creative destruction, 35
creativity, 47
crisis, 30–31
Crum, George, 55–56

D

Dalai Lama, 213–15, 223
deadlines, 198–99
death, fear of, 223–24, 227
decorum, 71, 82–83, 90, 237
deduction, 111, 115–22
definitions, 110–11, 126–28. *See also* framing
deliberative rhetoric, 41–42, 44–45, 109, 242
Democritus, 101
depression, 67
Descartes, René, 14
desire, 101–2, 225, 239–40

desire reversal, 101–2, 107
dilettantes, 63
divine punishment, fear of, 223, 227
Double Rainbow Guy, 225–26
doubt, 79
dramatic goodies, 198, 201
dynamical inspiration, 48

E

earthly goods, anxiety about, 224–25, 227
Ecclesiastes, 49
efficient cause, 112, 113, 122
emotions, 92–94, 238–40. *See also individual emotions*
enthymeme, 117–21, 123, 241
envy, 99–100, 106, 239
Epicureans/Epicureanism, 3, 221–25, 256–57
Epicurus of Samos, 221–22, 225
episodes, 191
essential elements, finding, 179
ethos, 77–91, 237–38
eudaimonia, 218–20
eunoia (Caring), 83–85, 87
event connections, 189–91, 200, 248
exigence, 40–41, 44, 50–52, 247
experimentation, 202–10

F

facts, 110–11
fad diets, 61
Fagels, Robert, 171
failure, 55–56, 88, 250
faking it, 81–83
fallacies, 134–40
false analogies, 137
Fates, 216–19
fear, 97–99, 104, 106, 239
figures, 162, 243–44
final cause, 112, 113, 122
fitness, 69–70
flaws, character, 198
focus, 134, 242
formal cause, 112, 113, 122
foundation beats, 195–98, 200–201
framing, 124–40, 220–22, 241
Franklin, Benjamin, 80, 96, 129, 156
friends with yourself, making, 83–85

G

gaps/gap mapping, 36–37, 44, 247
Gates, Bill, 39–40
Genesis, 127–28
Gilmore, Gary, 165
Gladwell, Malcolm, 60

goal setting, 4–7
God's punishment, fear of, 223, 227
good life, concept of, 220–21
Gorgias, 2, 94, 156–57, 159–60, 161, 167, 183
guilt, shame versus, 97

H
habit, 143–57, 242–43
happiness, 215–16, 218–22, 259
hasty generalizations, 137–38
Helen, 2
Heraclitus, 42
hero's journey, 192–94, 200, 248
Hill, Emily, 125–26
Homer, 18, 163, 171–72, 217
Horace, 31
humanism, 257–58
humor, 100–101, 106–7
humors, 105
hyperbole/Hyperbole, 60–73, 78, 226, 246

I
ideas, 49–50, 53–55. *See also* inspiration
implicit memory, 168
imposter syndrome, 88, 95, 114
induction, 111–15, 118, 122, 241
inspiration, 46–59, 249–50
interval training, 206
invention, 49–50, 56
irony, 62, 175–76, 245
isocolons, 164, 165–66
It's a Wonderful Life, 28–29

J
Jobs, Steve, 39, 49, 177
joy, 213–27
Jurek, Scott, 58

K
kairos, 25–45, 199, 246–48
Kairos (god), 35
kairotic moments, 33, 35–37
Kelly, R., 174
Kennedy, John F., 64
Kristofferson, Kris, 96
Kuhn, Thomas, 33

L
Lachesis, 217
Lamarr, Hedy, 79
lapse, using, 86–87
laughter, 100–101, 214–15, 239
liberality, 57, 59, 250
logic, 108–11, 240–42. *See also* deduction; induction

logos, 32–33, 108–23
long-term potentiation, 168
Lorenz, Edward, 34
love life, improving, 6–7, 71–72
Lucretius, 226
Lure & Ramp, 148–52, 157, 203, 242

M
magi, 161
major premises, 115–16
material cause, 111, 113, 122
Mayer, Louis B., 79
meanings, 127–28
mechanical inspiration, 48
Meditations (Aurelius), 221
Mellor, Reg, 133–34
metaphor, 62, 173–75, 183, 244
metonymy, 62, 172, 176–81, 183–84, 245
Midpoint, 196, 200, 249
mind, changing, 8
minor premises, 116
Miranda, Lin-Manuel, 177
models/modeling, 52–53, 58, 250
Mona Lisa, 22
Montaigne, Michel de, 53–54, 57
mood, changing, 7–8
moral inspiration, 48
Moses, Robert, 103

motivation, 8, 13–24, 92, 150
Mount Moosilauke running challenge, 68–69, 158, 202–10
movie star conundrum, 79–81
Musk, Elon, 21, 89, 126

N
napping, 7
narrative, 185–201, 258–59
Nature of Things, The (Lucretius), 226
needs versus wants, 22–24
neural prolotherapy, 204–5
neuroplasticity, 168
Newton, Isaac, 166
nostalgia cure, 42–44, 45, 247–48

O
Ochs, Adolph, 164
Odyssey (Homer), 18, 171–72, 217
Omnivore's Dilemma, The (Pollan), 147
On the Soul (Aristotle), 14, 92
opening in your mind, creating, 56–58
openings, looking for, 180
opportunities, 29–30, 31, 34–35, 38

P

paeans, 163–67, 168–71, 183, 204, 206, 243–44
pain, fear of, 224, 227
pain reframing, 131–32, 224. *See also* suffering
pathos, 92–107
Pauley, Jane, 125
peroration, 228–34
personal reality, mapping, 129–31
personalizing the issue, 130
persuadability, 94
persuasive moments, 30
pessimism bias, 43
philos, 84–85, 86–87, 90
phronesis, 87
pidgin thinking, 177–79, 181, 184, 245
pity, 133
Pizzagate, 187
placebo effect, 102–3, 174–75
Plato, 53, 94, 104, 124, 128
pleasure, friendship and, 84
plenary inspiration, 47–48
Plutarch, 125
Poetics (Aristotle), 186, 189
poetry/poetic prose, 161–62
polar bears, 109–10
Pollan, Michael, 147–48
post hoc, ergo propter hoc, 134–35
Poundstone, Paula, 147–48
Prefontaine, Steve, 132
Prior Analytics (Aristotle), 116
probabilities, 118
psychagogia (soul moving/bending), 2, 230
public speaking, 5–6, 70–71, 95
purpose, 230–31

R

Ramp, Lure &, 148–52, 203, 242
reality, differing, 158–60, 167, 183
receptivity, 94
redefining, 134, 242
refining, 54, 58–59, 250
repetition, effects of, 162, 165, 167–71, 183, 245
revision, 54
Rhetoric (Aristotle), 157, 160
rhetorical magnets, 78
rhythmic language, 161–62, 163–66
risk, 65

S

Saunders, George, 54
Save the Cat, 194–98, 200–201

schemes, 162
Schumpeter, Joseph, 34–35
scientific method, 34, 111
screenplays, 194–200
self-deprecating humor,
    100–101
self-mastery, 233–34
self-pity, 133
Serendib (Sri Lanka), 28, 32
serendipity, 28, 31, 32
Shakespeare, William, 63,
    161–62
shame, 20–21, 96–97, 106, 239
Silent Spring (Carson), 130
Silver, Spencer, 56
simplifying the topic, 130
sin recovery, 86–87, 91, 238
Six Things That Need Fixing,
    198, 201
skills, learning new, 5, 70
slogans, 163, 167–68, 244
snapping hip syndrome, 2,
    66–67
Snyder, Blake, 194, 197, 198
Socrates, 102, 126, 128, 231–32
Solon, 229
Sophists, 1–2, 8–9, 27, 31, 37,
    161, 215, 218, 254
soul
  Aristotle's concept of, 4, 14,
    16, 17, 128, 235–36
  as scout, 16–19
  syncing up with, 19–23
soul bending, introduction to,
    1–9
soul detector, 22, 236–37
speeches, giving, 5–6, 70–71, 95
Sputnik, 30
Star Wars, 188, 192
Stoics/Stoicism, 3, 220–21, 224,
    255–56
Stone Soup Method, 182
story, 248–49
storytelling, 185–201,
    258–59
strengths, playing up, 87–89
suffering, 103–4, 131–34,
    204–5, 208
Swift, Taylor, 16, 30, 180
Swim in a Pond in the Rain, A
    (Saunders), 54
syllogisms, 115–17
synecdoche, 62, 172, 181–83,
    184, 203, 245

T

temperance, 147
tetrapharmakos, 222–23,
    226–27
thaumaston, 225–26, 227
Thomas, Dylan, 229
Thoreau, Henry David, 66

thought-avoiding behavior, 93
"Three Princes of Serendib,
   The," 28
time, and kairos, 246–48
time, making adjustments for,
   153–56, 243
tool use, 232
Tortoise Method, 153, 155, 157,
   203, 243
Toulmin, Stephen, 34
Trojan War, 2
tropes, 162, 171–73,
   243–45
tying and untying, 189–91,
   193–94, 248

U

unit fallacy, 138–39
unrealistic optimism, 78
Unsoeld, Willi, 226
utility, friendship and,
   83–84

V

ventromedial prefrontal cortex,
   167
verbal inspiration, 47
virtue, 220–21
vision, 159

W

wants versus needs, 22–24
weight loss, 5, 36, 61, 69
West, Kanye, 30
White, Eric Charles, 32
Wieden, Dan, 165
Wilde, Oscar, 129
wit, Aristotle on, 6
witnessing, 148–49
words/language, 232–33,
   259–61
writing, 6

Z

Zeno of Citium, 221

ABOUT THE AUTHOR

JAY HEINRICHS is the *New York Times* bestselling author of *Thank You for Arguing*. He spent twenty-six years as a writer, editor, and magazine publishing executive before becoming a full-time advocate for the lost art of rhetoric. He now lectures widely on the subject, to audiences ranging from Ivy League students and NASA scientists to Southwest Airlines executives, and publishes the popular rhetoric newsletter *Aristotle's Guide to Soul Bending* on Substack. He lives with his wife in New Hampshire.